Algonquin Voices

Selected Stories of Canoe Lake Women

By Gaye I. Clemson

Printed in Victoria, Canada

National Library of Canada Cataloguing in Publication

Clemson, Gaye I. (Gaye Isabel), 1953-
    Algonquin voices : selected stories of Canoe Lake women / Gaye I. Clemson.

Includes bibliographical references.
ISBN 1-55369-489-9

    1. Women—Ontario—Canoe Lake—Biography. 2. Women—Ontario—Canoe Lake—History. 3. Canoe Lake (Ont.)—Biography. I. Title.

FC3065.A65C53 2002   971.3'147   C2002-901926-5
F1059.A4C53 2002

TRAFFORD

This book was published *on-demand* in cooperation with Trafford Publishing. On-demand publishing is a unique process and service of making a book available for retail sale to the public taking advantage of on-demand manufacturing and Internet marketing. **On-demand publishing** includes promotions, retail sales, manufacturing, order fulfilment, accounting and collecting royalties on behalf of the author.

Suite 6E, 2333 Government St., Victoria, B.C. V8T 4P4, CANADA
Order Desk (Toll-free) 1-866-752-6820

Phone	250-383-6864	Toll-free	1-888-232-4444 (Canada & US)
Fax	250-383-6804	E-mail	sales@trafford.com
Web site	www.trafford.com	TRAFFORD PUBLISHING IS A DIVISION OF TRAFFORD HOLDINGS LTD.	

Trafford Catalogue #02-0302   www.trafford.com/robots/02-0302.html

10   9   8   7   6   5   4   3

Cover and Chapter Watercolor Drawings by Mary Kendall Percival
Mary Kendall Percival is a longtime resident of Canoe Lake who first started
painting water colours at six years old from her family home in Muskoka.
She went on to study Commercial & Fine Arts, later moving to New York
City to add Illustration and Interior Design to her credentials. Mary's first
one-woman show was in New York, 1946. Since then Mary has sketched
and painted around the world. As a seasoned traveler, staying in many
uncommon habitations and locations with her husband Keith, Mary has
learned to appreciate unusual and natural wild places and she expresses
these visions through her artwork. Mary's first experience of Algonquin
was a result of a visit with the Northways at Nominigan in the 1920s. Her
father's friendship with Taylor Statten led to nine summers at Camp
Wapomeo as a counselor and teacher of leatherwork and art. Since 1947,
from her cabin in the stumpy, deadhead-packed bay behind Popcorn
Island, Mary has lovingly portrayed her vision of the Algonquin wilderness
through brush and colour.

Table of Contents

Dedication and Acknowledgements

In 1995, Bernard S. Shaw wrote a book about Canoe Lake in Algonquin Park that provided great insight into the history of the area. He described in detail the logging era and the life and mystery of Tom Thomson, a famous Canadian painter who died on the lake under mysterious circumstances in 1917. However, little mention was made of the over 80 leasehold residents and their families who have called Canoe Lake their home since the turn of the century. As one of these residents, I was inspired by Mr. Shaw's work to find out more about my lakeside neighbours. For four summers I avidly collected oral histories from everyone on the lake. I learned about their settlement motivations and lots of wonderful stories about the weather, animals, boats, canoe trips, artistic endeavours, interesting characters, family traditions and weekend amusements. I discovered that for some, the family roots were with the various lumbering operations at Mowat, the railroad or the Department of Lands and Forests (now called the Ministry of Natural Resources). Many others came to Canoe Lake because they had attended one of the Taylor Statten Camps. Some just appeared, perhaps after having visited friends or one of the many resorts in the area, fell in love with the place and never left.

What became very clear after awhile, was that I was assembling a large number of narratives about a marvelous collection of courageous mothers, grandmothers, aunts, sisters and cousins that needed a voice. These women came from a wide variety of backgrounds and their rich, vivid and heartfelt stories needed to be told. Some were married to husbands who loved the outdoors and came with their children to spend their summers in the wilderness. Many others were widowed, divorced, or single and had a passion for Algonquin Park that overcame remarkable difficulties. I had written about one of the most awesome of these women in an earlier book, "Gertrude Baskerville—The Lady of Algonquin Park," published in 2001. She lived alone on Tea Lake for over 35 years. This second book is my attempt to capture and bring to life the voices of another collection of women. It is not intended to be a history of each person, but just a reflection to the reader of a few aspects of their lives on Canoe Lake.

I must first thank all of the families of all of the people represented here for their kindness in sharing their experiences and their contributions of photographs and anecdotes. I am deeply indebted to the Lewis Family, Catherine Thompson Brackley, Isobel Cowie, Mary Colson Clare, Sue Ebbs, Mary Margaret Armstrong Withey, the late Islay McFarlane and Don Standfield, for sharing with the Ministry of Natural Resources Archives the transcripts of interviews he conducted with various Algonquin Park residents for his book, "Algonquin: the Park and Its People." A special thanks must also go to Ron Tozer, retired Park naturalist/archivist, and Chris Boettger, the current archivist at the Algonquin Park Visitor Center, who welcomed me warmly and facilitated access to the Park archives and personnel. All were most helpful in pointing me in the right direction for some of the early records and photographs. Last but not least, I'll be forever grateful to Joanne Clark for her skill in graphics and layout and Mark Hammond whose editing talents were awesome. Enjoy!!!!

• • • • • • • •

Poem by Mary Wilson Hayhurst[1]

The rain-washed earth sweet incense lifts
Through the morning air, ascending;
And into my heart a longing drifts
For the scent that the bracken is sending.
To be in the mist that lies on the lake,
With the whir of the reel a-singing;
To watch the rings in the water break,
Where the gleaming trout is springing.
To see the shrouded, wraith-like forms
Of the trees in the early morning,
When the spirit of night, its passing mourns,
And, breathless, Nature waits for the dawning.
To watch the white mist turn to gold,
And the red sun, upward climbing;
A wizard he-the mists unfold,
Familiar lake and pine divining.
To smell the smoke on the woodland air,
The coffee 's tang, and the bacon frying,
To find their red coals waiting there
For the fish in your stout net lying.
To feast, while through the depths of blue
The giant crane his way is winging;
On every bush a lover true,
To the heart of his mate is singing.
Oh, what is the lure of the city street
When the sprite of the north is calling,
To come where the sky and the forest meet,
In the joy of a dew-drenched morning!

---

[1] Mary Wilson Hayhurst and her husband Thomas Haywood Hayhurst were one of the first "official" Canoe Lake leaseholders having settled on Canoe Lake in 1908. Thomas was born in the United Kingdom, but grew up in Hamilton and had contracted a weakness of the lungs. They were friends of the Piries and Bertrams on Gilmour Island. They came because Dr. Bertram had suggested that time amongst the evergreens would be good for healing Thomas's lungs. They both fell in love with Canoe Lake and decided to settle on a point at the north end, across from the town of Mowat on what is now called Hayhurst Point. Thomas and Mary had five children Thomas Edward, George, Alexander, William and Jean. Thomas Edward was killed at Dieppe in WWII. Alexander died of black throat diphtheria in 1915 and was buried in the Canoe Lake cemetery. Mary was an accomplished poetess and was published frequently in the Toronto Star and other local Ontario newspapers. She died suddenly at the early age of 54.

Prologue

My profession as a high tech marketing strategist means that I live 11 months of the year in northern California, but the trek for me to Canoe Lake each summer is relatively painless. Direct flights to Toronto from San Francisco now enable the entire trip to be completed in about 10 hours. A five-hour early morning flight arrives at Pearson airport around 3:30 p.m. Though there are sometimes delays in getting baggage and negotiating customs and immigration, most of the time my rental car and I can be motoring north on Highway 400 within the hour. If I've timed the rush hour traffic correctly, I can reach the bustling town of Huntsville in a little over two hours. Quick stops at Robinson's Independent for groceries, the Huntsville Canadian Tire for any needed supplies for the annual cottage "Joe Job List," and Henrietta's Bakery for Nanaimo bars, fresh bread, pies, butter tarts and the obligatory sausage rolls usually takes an hour or so. From Huntsville, a short 40-minute drive has me picking up my summer parking pass at the Algonquin Park gates. At the 14-kilometer post I turn north off Highway 60 onto the Portage Store access road. A few hundred yards down the road a quick right takes me down a steep hill that skirts past the Canoe Lake Permit office, nestled on the sandy beach at the bottom of Portage Bay. The road then continues up the eastside of the bay to the Canoe Lake leaseholders' dock.

From this end, Canoe Lake looks deceptively small. It seems long and thin, and several islands in the middle of the lake block the view of the large expanse of water at the north end. It's actually four kilometers long and about one kilometer wide at its widest point. To the west runs Whiskey Jack Creek, an oasis of nature for birds and a respite for loons from the noise and chaos of the lake. Moose can often be seen at dusk feeding on the fine swamp vegetation. To the south runs Bonita Narrows which connects Canoe Lake to Tea Lake and Smoke Lake beyond. But it isn't until a visitor gets out of Portage Bay that the lake's haunting beauty becomes apparent. On both shores the land rises quite sharply from the water's edge, its steepness masked by the dense hardwood forest. In several spots huge granite cliffs provide glorious lookouts and marvelous sun bathing spots. Only on the northeast shore, in a sheltered bay, is there any expanse of sandy beach.

At the leaseholders' dock I fold myself out of the car and stretch. The twittering sounds of the birds in the forest to my left engulf me. I pause and I hear the crickets and bullfrogs echoing from the swampy part of Portage Bay behind me. I feel a strange light-headedness as I gaze across the small bay to the Portage Store. I can see the staff putting away the last of the canoes, life jackets and paddles used by returning canoeists and trippers. The few remaining restaurant visitors sit with their ice cream cones on the upper deck by the gift shop admiring the view. The lake is calm with only the occasional spider bug disturbing its glassy surface. I take a deep breath of the fresh, pungent forest, its fine smells of cedar, pine and hemlock mixed in with wet leaves and the earthy redolence of the swamp. My vision blurs and for a moment I can see the reflection of the old store in the water just as the sun goes down. Molly is out on the verandah sweeping out the vestiges of the day's visitors, and her husband Ed is replacing the burlap over the cedar strip canoes that rest on a bed of straw down by the shore. From the storeroom around the back comes the laughter of a group of women. Isobel, Marg, Janey and Fran are closing up for the day. The sun dips below the tree line and all is cast in shadows. I blink and the images are gone.

I stop daydreaming and refocus on the task at hand. Arrival at the leaseholders' dock is just the beginning of what is the most arduous part of the trek. Everything in the car needs to be unloaded and reloaded into the boat. My family's little aluminum boat with its 9.9-horsepower Yamaha engine awaits me quietly, right where the local handyman had left it earlier in the day. It's broad in the beam, which is great for moving gear and supplies but terribly hard to maneuver in a stiff wind. On a bad day, I long for the wooden cedarstrip boat that we used to have when I was a kid. I gaze at the car and marvel once more at my genetic ability to pack so much in it – a gift my brother and I inherited from my father. After a half an hour of grunting and groaning to myself, everything is safely stowed in the boat. I start up the engine with a couple of hard pulls on the starter cord and steer the boat north out of Portage Bay. Once clear of what was once Rimmer Point I set a course directly west into the remains of the setting sun.

On any given day there can be dozens of canoes on the lake rented out by the Portage Store outfitting department. Many of these canoeists head straight north to do some interior canoe tripping, up the east shore past Braucht's Lighthouse. Others are just day visitors who venture out onto the lake to test their novice paddling skills. Some of these visitors know of Tom Thomson and the mystery of his death. They stop for a picnic or rest at his totem pole and cairn perched on a high cliff near Hayhurst Point. Most though are oblivious to the history of the lake around them. As they look out or paddle across the lake they may or may not notice the gaggle of cottages that hug the western shore. This is all that remains of a vibrant logging community that was the town of Mowat at the turn of the century. Only the really knowledgeable and hardy know how to find the Canoe Lake Cemetery on the hill beyond the original Mowat town site. An ancient birch tree still protects the spot where Tom Thomson rested for awhile on his journey to the spirit world.

A few enterprising canoeists will now and again reach the north end of the lake and venture up the meandering stream to the west called Potter Creek. Several solitary cabins hug the shore at the mouth of the creek and give a hint of the little community that used to inhabit the spot year-round for more than 50 years, from 1893 to about the beginning of World War II. Further north the remains of a large wooden trestle bridge that once crossed the creek can be seen. There are no signs of the train station, baggage chute and docking area once located at the spot where the creek narrows and runs under what is now the access road to Arowhon Pines Resort. Only those who are very observant will notice the broad meadows on the west shore now full of scrub spruce trees covering what was once miles and miles of railroad siding, or the occasional stone fireplace standing stark against the blue sky. Only those who are adventurous dare step through the woods to discover the remains of what was once a huge lumber mill, which hugged the shore during the 1930s and '40s. A few others venture to Joe Lake Dam for a picnic and a swim. They are oblivious to the yesteryear bustle of the train station, hotel and outfitting store—pillars of the lake community until the late 1950s and now disappeared.

After about a half-mile or so, I turn the boat south and look for the high cliff face on the east shore just past Buffalo Point. It's easy to spot, even at night, because of a stand of birch trees and a tall pine tree that grow at water's edge. Once I reach the dock, I jump out and tie up the boat. Several years ago, in my eagerness to reach the dock, I forgot this step and was shocked to see my neighbour to the north arriving for a visit several hours later with my boat in tow behind them. They had been sitting out on their deck admiring the setting sun, when low and behold our boat went drifting past their dock like a piece of flotsam on the sea. The story of their rescue of the boat and my resulting embarrassment provided the rest of the lake with a great story that got embellished and embroidered for most of that summer.

Everything in the boat now must be unloaded onto the dock. This is done with great enthusiasm. I pause for a moment mid-task to survey the path upwards and listen to the sound of the boat's wake lapping the shoreline. The images of Jean Pirie, Jennie Armstrong, Margaret Hayhurst and Amy Loyst busily super-vising this same activity come to mind. A summer's worth of luggage, goods, provisions and supplies must now be hauled up the cliff. It's a distance of about 50 vertical feet, which translates to about 75 switchback paces. Not much of a distance in the scheme of things, but our own little Mount Everest none the less. I remember with a chuckle the first time that I came up with my two young twin sons, Kristopher and Taylor, five years ago. They were 2 years old and though walking steadily, the climb over rocks and roots to the top was a chal-lenge. However, once we got there, I realized that I couldn't just leave them atop the hill while I returned to the dock to haul up the rest of the provisions and supplies. Neither the cabin nor the verandah was child-proof, so the only solu-tion was to attach the harnesses they were wearing to a rope strung between two large trees. It worked like a charm. In this way they could run freely up and down the length of rope and not be in any danger of falling off the deck or into the lake or wandering off into the forest.

My first few trips up the path are always done full of great energy. One by one the cases of beer and wine, the boxes and bags of food and canned goods, the luggage and the Canadian Tire supplies are hauled up the hill. Later my breath-ing gets a bit laboured. After a dozen or so trips my legs start to ache. For some reason my arms never get tired. They must have memory of all of the years of canoe tripping and paddling, so can stand the strain. Finally the entire mound of goods and equipment has been hauled up to the verandah, and safely sorted into cupboard, refrigerator and closet. It's time now for a cold drink and if the weather is good and the water warm, a quick jump in the lake to cool off. As I take in the last rays of the setting sun dancing and sparkling on the water from my bench on the dock, I think about the lives of the many women who have called Canoe Lake their summer home during the past century. Their voices echo vibrantly in my mind. Voices that until now, have been trapped in the dusty records of libraries, archives, family photo albums and the lost corners of drawers and memories. I grab my pen and paper and start writing.

View of Canoe Lake from South Bay, 1953—
APMA #1269 J. Leech Porter

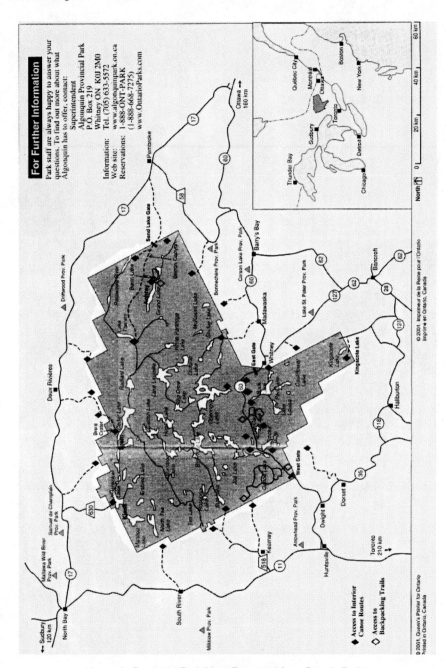

Algonquin Provincial Park Map, Excerpted from Ontario Parks
Publication #5021—Printed by Friends of Algonquin Park

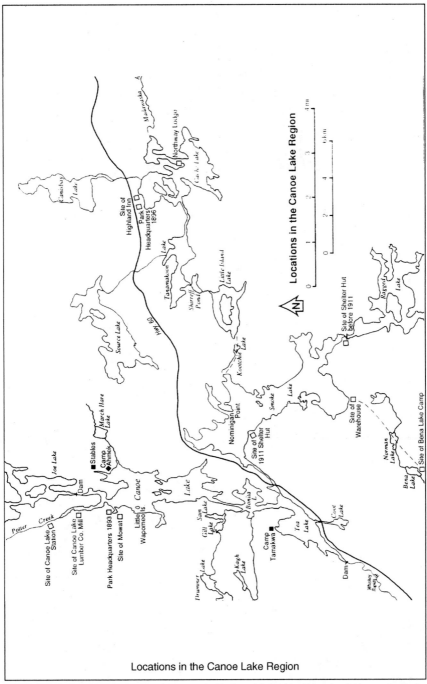

Locations in the Canoe Lake Region

Source: G.D. Garland, Glimpses of Algonquin Park, published by Friends of Algonquin Park, 1989, pg. 9.

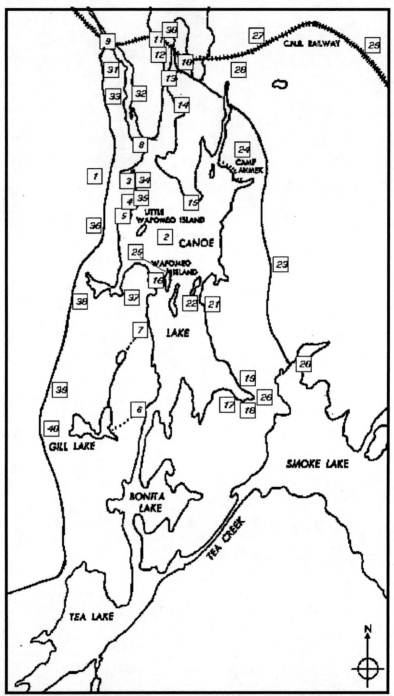

Canoe Lake in Algonquin Park Map—Modified from a map found in The Tom Thomson Mystery by William Little, published by McGraw-Hill Company of Canada Ltd., 1970.

Map Label Key

1. Canoe Lake Cemetery
2. Tom Thomson's Body Found
3. Mowat Lodge I
4. Trainor Cottage
5. Blecher Cottage
6. Gill Lake Portage
7. Alternate Gill Lake Portage
8. Lawrie Dickson's cabin
9. Canoe Lake Station
10. Mark Robinson's Cabin
11. Algonquin Hotel
12. Colson's Store
13. Joe Lake Dam
14. Favourite Thomson Camp Site
15. Tom Thomson Totem Pole and Cairn
16. Tom Thomson's Canoe Found
17. Portage Store
18. MNR Permit Office
19. Leaseholder's Dock
20. Smoke Lake Hanger
21. Lighthouse Point
22. Cook's Island
23. Arowhon Road
24. Camp Ahmek
25. Camp Wapomeo
26. Leaseholder Garages
27. Taylor Statten Station
28. Sim's Pit
29. Ottawa, Arnprior and Parry Sound Railway Line
30. Joe Lake Station
31. Canoe Lake School
32. Trestle Bridge
33. Lumber Company Remains
34. Mowat Town Site and Chip Yard
35. Gilmour Mill/Park Headquarters/Mowat Lodge II
36. Gilmour Hospital
37. Canoe Lake Dump
38. Canoe Lake Farm
39. Gilmour Road
40. Gilmour Lumber Camp

ALGONQUIN VOICES

Chapter 1
The Pioneers

The Pioneers

My neighbours, Nick and Debbie, have invited us over for a swim and dinner. Their cabin is called "Edgemere," named by one of the Hayhurst children who owned it for many years. Besides the Gilmour residences, it is probably the oldest cabin still standing on the lake. It's made of squared-off logs and sits out over the water but looks strangely out of place. This is because it sits squished between the Blecher property to the south and "The Manse" to the north. There is no bumper lot between them as is the practice on other parts of Canoe Lake. This is quite unusual and makes for cozy relationships with neighbours. Historical records show that it was likely one of the original Gilmour outbuildings, sold in 1910 to a Mr. C. O. Anderson by a Reverend Turk. Turk owned most of the property in the surrounding area having likely obtained the buildings from the Gilmour receivers. In those days, no one seemed to really pay much attention to the underlying land lease arrangements. This became a major problem for Anderson later as the Department of Lands and Forests had no record of his existence and deed transfer from Turk.[2]

I duck under the low doorframe and enter Edgemere's small kitchen. Near the sink is an inactive water pump, a small fridge and stove. Just off the kitchen is a very quaint living room with an airtight stove and two small bedrooms tucked off to the side. Out back is an outhouse and a pathway into the forest. If I look carefully I can see the remains of a large gate that must have blocked the cabin off from the access road that connected these cabins to the railway line. Looking next door, I can see that nothing is left of the old two-story Blecher place that used to be there. A new cabin built a few summers ago sits back from the shoreline. It is much smaller than the building it replaced and the forest hasn't yet had a chance to creep in, so the cabin looks like it doesn't belong. Nothing remains of the old boathouse where Martin Blecher kept his workshop and his boat and in later life lived with his second wife.

---

[2] The lease title didn't get sorted out until 1919 when the property lines was grandfathered, which is why there is no "bumper" lot between this cabin and its neighbours.

Louisa Blecher has been dead for over 50 years, but the aura of her presence is still palpable in the forest shadows. In my mind's eye, the big "No Trespassing" sign Louisa had once hung outside her home to ward off would-be visitors leaps out of the forest. The ghosts of the family seem to haunt the area and even now it oozes mystery and darkness. I creep along the path, almost fearful that Louisa will appear and chase me off with her broom as she did Mark Robinson, the local park ranger. He had come to tell her once again, that she was flying her American flag in an unapproved way. The remains of the path weave past the cottage and dead ends in a small clearing. It's quite boggy and wet, but the view from here is spectacular. I can see the Tom Thomson totem pole and cairn right across the lake, as well as Hayhurst Point, where Mary Hayhurst had composed numerous poems published in magazines and newspapers in the 1920s.

I can hear the sounds of children's laughter from the Camp Wapomeo waterfront and see the clearing on Little Wapomeo Island where Tonakela and the Chief set up their teepee so long ago. Just out of the corner of my eye is the top of the roof of "The Loon's Retreat" at the south end of Gilmour Island. Another image of Louisa chastising her neighbours, with her son looking on, passes through my eyes. I shiver and head back to the little cabin for a glass of red wine and some fine storytelling.

Jean Bertram Pirie

Jean Bertram Pirie with Dr. Alexander Pirie
circa 1910—Lewis Collection

Jean Bertram Pirie

During the summer of 1905, Jean Bertram Pirie's husband, Dr. Alexander Pirie, and his close friend Dr. Thomas Bertram (Jean's uncle), decided to take a canoe trip through Algonquin Park. While paddling north up Canoe Lake they discovered two abandoned houses on the south end of an island in the middle of the lake. Both frame houses were more than 1700 square feet in size and looked as if they had been unoccupied for at least a half a dozen years. Both were sturdily built with brick and stone fireplaces and plastered walls, and had been winterized for year-round occupancy with double-planked floors. Though the shoreline was desolate and uninviting, Dr. Pirie was enamoured by Canoe Lake and decided to investigate the history and ownership of the buildings and see if they were for sale. At the time, Dr. Pirie, a native of the Dundas area near Hamilton, was living in Costa Rica where he had been practicing medicine since 1887. In addition to his medical practice, he also owned several plantations that grew coffee, bananas and sugar. Dr. Pirie started asking around and discovered that David and Allan Gilmour, owners of the Gilmour Lumber Company of Trenton, Ontario had built the houses. The two brothers had also built a now bankrupt saw and planing mill (Canoe Lake Mills) on the northwest shores of Canoe Lake near what was then the town of Mowat. The Gilmours' Canoe Lake experiences was quite the story.[3]

It seemed that in 1892, the Ontario government had sold to David Gilmour, through a public auction in Toronto, the logging rights to an area southwest and north of Canoe Lake. For the astronomical sum of $703,875 and an annual rent of $270, Gilmour won the rights to almost 87 square miles of huge pine and hardwood forests. He and his brother Allan immediately set up logging camps along the Oxtongue River, the main waterway within their limit, which connected Dorset to the outskirts of Algonquin Park. According to an article in an 1895 edition of the Bobcaygeon Independent newspaper, the Gilmour Lumber Company had 11 camps, each of which housed 55 men and 150 pairs of horses. Sixty-five "cadge" teams hauled supplies all winter up and down the "tote" road. The Gilmours extended this road to Tea Lake, just inside their timber limits. Here they established a supply depot and administrative headquarters. It wasn't long before every

---

[3] For the details of this history, please see Shaw, B., *Canoe Lake Algonquin Park – Tom Thomson and Other Mysteries*, General Store Publishing House, Burnstown, 1996.

white pine of any size in the area had been cut down and hauled to the Oxtongue River.

Logging was much different in the 1890s than it had been in the 1830s, when the first loggers had come through the area. In the 1830s loggers would go over the same ground repeatedly, taking out only the best trees every few years. But in the 1890s the common practice was to clear-cut anything over 10 feet tall with cross cut saws. The result:

> "Felling of every pine tree meant the maiming and destruction of several other trees and the aggregate loss entailed by these operations in the forest wealth of the limits was very large."[4]

Crosscutting did have a few advantages. One was that much less wood was wasted. Three men would work together and cut the trees much closer to the ground than they could with axes. One man would measure and the other two men would handle the saw. A three-person team was expected to cut 65 logs a day. The measurer would put a cut 4 to 5 inches deep on the underside, which would indicate the direction in which the tree would fall. After the tree was down, he would mark out where additional cuts needed to be made on the fallen tree. The rate of pay was according to skill. New loggers could expect to earn about 50 cents a day plus board. A "square off" expert could earn $1 a day, as could a "cutter" with his or her own horse. The pay at the Gilmour Lumber Company in 1897 was estimated to be $1.50 a day.[5]

To make some of the smaller waterways more navigable and store the water used to help flush logs down the Oxtongue River, Gilmour constructed dams in 1893-94 at Joe and Tea Lakes. The water level of the surrounding lakes rose a good two feet, devastating the shoreline. Smoke, Canoe and Tea Lakes became connected together into one continuous waterway. Alligators (flat-bottomed scows with side-mounted paddle wheels and a powerful winch to haul logs on water) and pointers (long shallow-draught row boats with points at both ends to transport men and supplies) were brought in from Lake of Bays to ply the three-lake water system. All of the little

---

[4] Garland, G.D., (compiler) *Glimpses of Algonquin Park*, Friends of Algonquin Park, Algonquin Park, pg. 49.

[5] Addison, O., *Early Days in Algonquin Park*, McGraw-Hill, Ryerson, Toronto, 1974, pg. 10.

bays became wastelands of stumps and sunken logs. Over the years, the landscape became desolate and gray as thousands of trees along the shore died. Three peninsulas became little islands and the big island in the center of Canoe Lake became two separate islands once the Department of Lands and Forests built a permanent dam some years later.[6]

In order to have a place to stay during their visits, the Gilmours built the two large residences on the end of the southern most island.[7] This location was within easy reach of the logging camp that they had established on the northwest shore of the lake right next to Algonquin Park Headquarters. The Park Headquarters remained on Canoe Lake until 1897 when it was moved to Cache Lake. It's not clear in the records as to why this change was made. Some think that it may have been that Cache Lake's more central location made supervision of the Park easier. Cache Lake was also much more picturesque, likely another factor. The Department did maintain a smaller "shelter house" at Canoe Lake, which from 1899 to 1909 functioned as a park sub-headquarters. In 1909 the sub-headquarters moved to "The Manse" nearby, allegedly named after a Presbyterian Minister who would stay there when in Mowat to conduct church services. This cabin was really a way station for visiting rangers and was used for that purpose until 1911.

Once Dr. Pirie discovered that the two houses on the island were for sale, he contacted the Gilmour Lumber Company receiver and soon bought them for $1,150. With this purchase also came another building on Potter Creek known then as the "Souler House." At one time it had been the main check point for supplies entering the mill site and for lumber being shipped out.[8] Dr. Pirie had no interest in using it so it was soon sold to W. T. Insley under a lease-to-purchase arrangement. Dr. Pirie named the seven-bedroom main Gilmour cottage "The Loon's Retreat" and Dr. Bertram was granted free use of the other, smaller, four bedroom house, which in the 1930s became know as "Uncle Tom's Cabin." The next year, 1906, Dr. Pirie applied to Park Superintendent George Bartlett for a lease for Gilmour Island. At the time, a local official advised him that everything was in order and that, "If the government wished to communicate anything further they would do so in due course."[9]

---

[6] The bigger islands are now called Pirie's or Gilmour Island and Big Wapomeo Island; the smaller ones are called Little Wapomeo, Chubby's and Popcorn.
[7] The family's best guess is that the houses were built in the 1897-98 time period. Some Algonquin Park records have suggested that it was much earlier, but there is no confirmation.
[8] *Early Days in Algonquin Park*, pg. 22.
[9] Letter to the Deputy Minister of Lands and Forests dated 1926.

No further official correspondence was received, so Dr. Pirie assumed that his agreement with the Gilmour receiver was acceptable to the Department of Lands and Forests. Later correspondence was found between Bartlett and others asking if there were any objections to issuing a lease, but records of the time do not show that an official lease was ever issued.[10]

Dr. Pirie's brother, Edwin Pirie, a lawyer who acted on Dr. Pirie's behalf in these matters, couldn't understand what the appeal of Canoe Lake was to his brother. In his view, Canoe Lake held no charm at all—at least compared to Georgian Bay. As he wrote at the time,

> "A small inland lake with all sorts of difficulty to reach it, has no charm for me at all. Take away the boy's camp and the lake would relapse into its pristine isolation and dreariness, with the roughest of shores. It is unclear to me what on earth there is there that would induce anyone to waste the good old summertime there."[11]

The lease issue didn't surface again until 1926 when the Ontario provincial tax collector questioned the family's rights to the property. The Department of Lands and Forests could find no files or letters on record pertaining to the Pirie holdings. But after some lawyerly intervention and much correspondence, the matter was eventually resolved and in 1927 an official lease was issued to Dr. Pirie and Dr. Bertram.[12]

In 1907, Dr. Pirie married Jean Bertram and with their growing family would visit Canoe Lake occasionally. But it wasn't until the 1920s that extended visits to their Canoe Lake summer home became an integral part of the family's activities. By then, there were five children in the family who spent their winters at various boarding schools. Jean and Dr. Pirie wanted a wholesome spot where they could gather the entire clan together each summer for an extended period. Canoe Lake proved to be ideal, but getting there was a challenge. In June each year, Dr. and Mrs. Pirie would arrive at their Dundas family home from Costa Rica. Before heading north

---

[10]Ministry of Natural Resources lease archives. The lack of correspondence from this period may also have been due to a fire about that time that destroyed many early Algonquin Park records.

[11]Pirie Family correspondence.

[12]Dr. Bertram resigned his interest in the lease in 1948.

to Algonquin Park, the couple would spend a day at Eaton's in Toronto ordering and testing supplies. All equipment and supplies for the two months had to be packed and shipped by train to Canoe Lake Station. The family would take a local bus to the Dundas Canadian National Railway station, and board a train for an hour's ride to Union Station in Toronto. Here they would wait until midnight to board the northbound sleeper train. Once they reached Scotia Junction, they would have to wait again for the eastbound "Ottawa, Arnprior and Parry Sound" train, which would drop them off at Canoe Lake Station early the next morning. From there, they would be rowed down the lake to the island. Dr. Bertram, when he was in his 80s, told one leaseholder that a common practice was to fashion a makeshift raft by lashing a platform between two canoes and in this way transport their supplies down to the island. After arriving at the cottage, the supplies were unpacked and placed in a downstairs storage room for use during the summer. All of the kids would look forward to the opening of the supply boxes.

Jean Pirie was a tremendously well-organized, energetic, hard-working and courageous person. She was a graduate of Queen's University at Kingston circa 1905 at a time when few women had the opportunity or desire to attend institutes of higher education. Not only did she leave her comfortable surroundings in Canada and immigrate to Costa Rica (likely very primitive at that time) but she was willing to come to the Canadian wilderness every summer. She lived and managed a household with no running water and only kerosene lamps for light. She fed and kept clean and healthy a vast group of family and visitors. The family kept chickens in a "chicken house" that today houses firewood. One year her mother-in-law (known as Grandma Pirie) borrowed a cow to supply milk for the season from the Frasers at Mowat Lodge.[13] Mealtimes were always a highlight, though cooking three meals a day for a minimum of 10 people must have been a monumental task. Every stick of wood had to be sawn and split and all hot foods had to be cooked or baked on a cast iron wood stove. To assemble everyone for dinner, Jean, known as Nana by the family in later life, rigged up a dinner gong that could be heard for miles around. A few moments after dinner was the only time that she was able to relax. She would sit out on the front porch in a swinging chair suspended from the ceiling. Evenings would be spent playing bridge, reading, knitting and chatting with the assembled family.

---

[13]Details as to the Fraser's and their life running Mowat Lodge may be found in Chapter 2.

Every day had a major household task associated with it. Monday was wash day. Tuesday was ironing day and Wednesday was bread and pie-baking day. Jean had a large wooden tub with a large handle that needed to be cranked to agitate the water. She figured that it would take about 100 cranks to ensure that all of the clothes were clean. The clothes then had to be scrubbed on the scrub boards, rinsed and then hung out to dry. Once dry, she had old flatirons that she would heat up to press the clothes. The smaller children were in charge of keeping the firebox well supplied with wood. They also had to make sure that every day the icebox was cleaned and loaded with a new block of ice. In the early years the ice was likely bought either from the Algonquin Hotel or Mowat Lodge. In later years the Portage Store took over this function. The family would often go on berry picking picnic expeditions to Tea Lake or Smoke Lake. On Sunday all of the family members were required to dress in their "Sunday best" and gather at Uncle Tom's Cabin. They would sing hymns and listen to organ music, usually played by Mrs. Thomas Bertram (known as Aunt Bert). Dr. Pirie would give the sermon. They also had a comprehensive set of "Rules of Behaviour"—some of them tongue-in-cheek—to which all family and visitors had to abide.

Today Jean's grandchildren and great-grandchildren continue to own and maintain the two houses. The entire Pirie clan numbers in the hundreds, and they still get together periodically at Canoe Lake. In 1993, to coincide with the 100-year anniversary of the park's founding, the family held a huge reunion on the island complete with custom-made T-shirts. Jean Pirie continued to visit Canoe Lake each summer until 1957. She was bedridden until her death in 1965 but would often long for her summer Canoe Lake home.

Gilmour Depot at Tea Lake in Winter—APMA #1093 MNR Hist. #19

Gilmour's Canoe Lake Mills, 1903—APMA #7108 Elizabeth Osborne

Panorama of Canoe Lake Station Looking West,
circa 1920s—APMA #5905 Helen Jones

Canoe Lake Station—APMA #2039 Ottelyn Addison

Gilmour Island, circa 1910—Lewis Collection

Loons' Retreat, circa 1980s—Lewis Collection

Grandma Bertram (l) and Grandma Pirie (r) Hard at Work,
circa 1930s—Lewis Collection

Jean Pirie Out for an Evening Paddle—Lewis Collection

Jean and Dr. Pirie with their Grandson, Sandy Lewis,
1940—Lewis Collection

Family Portrait by the Wood Pile,
(L to R) Margaret Pirie (Dr. Pirie's mother), Mary
Robieson Pirie, Children—Jean Margaret Pirie (back),
Alex Bertram Pirie and Mary Isobel Pirie (front)

Pirie Family Rules of Behaviour, circa 1910

	Rules	Exceptions	Penalties
1	Thou shall not booze.		Soaked in the drink (i.e. the lake)
2	Smoking allowed at all times except in bed. No cigarettes allowed.	Boys under 20, allowed one pipe a day.	Any person breaking this rule will not be allowed to smoke or even smell smoke for one day.
3	No swearing allowed.	Except when you stub your toe or lose a good fish, and then in an underbreath only	Saw wood
4	Lights out at 10:30 p. m.	Except when the train is late	Buy a dozen candles or a gallon of coal oil
5	Top flat reserved for ladies	Jamie allowed on Top Flat	A pail of cold water
6	No borrowing of each other's chewing juice	Except in cases of emergency	Chew the rag
7	All photographs must pass inspection by the chaperone before being made public	Except on Sundays	Camera will be taken away
8	All post cards are public property and must be put in the rack at once	No exception	Confiscation, next letter will be held
9	No stylish clothes allowed	Except new arrivals on their first day	Portage the canoe to Smoke Lake
10	Bathing Rules: Time limit 1/2 hour, 1/4 hour preferred		Can't go in for a week
11	Any eggs found on the Island outside of the chicken house are public property		
12	No more than one allowed in the hammock at once	Engaged couples excepted	Bump their heads together
13	All must attend church on Sunday mornings	No exceptions	Must read Sunday sermon & say grace for a week
14	Dignity of the house must be maintained, no familiarity		
15	No snoring		A clothes-pin
16	Every person must be on time for meals	Except where business prevents	Go without
17	Girls must not go out in the boats alone unless reporting to headquarters		Must wash dishes for a day
18	Rules maybe amended or added to by 2/3 vote of the Birds		
19	Guests must register within 24 hours of arrival		Banishment from Loon's Retreat
20	Women not allowed on West side of house or grounds before breakfast	Only with consent of the boys the night before	
21	Baskets are on the verandah & in the house for waste paper & other waste material		Anyone found depositing waste elsewhere will be fined.

Louisa Blecher

(L to R) Louisa Blecher, Albert Wilkinson,
Mrs. & Mr. Edwin Thomas—APMA #0050 Jack Wilkinson

Louisa Blecher

Louisa Blecher arrived at Canoe Lake from Buffalo in 1909 with her husband Martin H. Blecher Sr., and two grown children, Martin Jr. and Bessie. Of German descent, the Blechers bought a parcel of land that included several buildings and a boathouse from Reverend George Turk. The main cabin was a two-story white washed wood-framed cottage with green trim. It had four bedrooms upstairs and all the inside walls were lathed and plastered, which was quite unusual for the time. The family would arrive each year early in the spring and to stay late into the fall. Martin Sr. had apparently made some money in the furniture business in the USA and was now retired. Bessie was an elementary school assistant principal. Some locals thought Martin Jr. was a private detective during the winter months because he didn't seem to have a paying job except for occasional work around the lake fixing boats and small engines. He was a wizard with machinery and had a lot of expensive tools that he would keep in his boathouse.

After the onset of World War I, there was in Canada a tremendous amount of ill will directed at those of German heritage. The Blechers were also American and, for many Canadians, Americans were always suspect. As a result, they were treated with a great deal of suspicion. What made matters worse was the fact that Martin Blecher Sr. was apparently somewhat gruff and hard to get along with. This all meant that the Blechers seem to have kept very much to themselves. At one point there was even some talk on the lake that Blecher Jr. was a German spy. There is of course no evidence to prove this assertion, but it is an urban legend that has been passed down ever since. Matters were not helped with the death of Tom Thomson in 1917.

Tom Thomson was a Canadian artist with a new style of painting that depicted northern landscapes with emotional depth and vivid colours, a departure from the art form prevalent in Canada at the time. He had been coming to Mowat Lodge to paint in the Park since 1914, and today many of his works are displayed at museums all over Canada. To supplement his meager painting income, he would often get odd jobs around the lake and guide fishing parties. Allegedly Tom and Martin Blecher Jr. were both interested in one of the local girls, Winifred Trainor, whose father, Hugh, a lumber foreman, had taken over the "The Manse" lease in 1909. On the morning of July 8, 1917, Tom departed on a fishing expedition and was never seen alive again. The next day Martin Jr. and his sister Bessie, on their way to Tea Lake Dam, had seen Tom's canoe floating upside down but didn't report it until much later. They claimed they hadn't known Tom was missing nor recognized his canoe. In hindsight this is hard to believe since Thomson's canoe had been painted a very unique shade of gray-green. In addition, it was a long-standing tradition (and still is today) that every Canoe Lake community member's watercraft be instantly recognizable.

On July 16, two local handymen and fellow guides, George Rowe and Lawrie Dickson, found and recovered Tom's body with the help of a Dr. Howland, who was staying on Little Wapomeo Island. Tom's body was floating in the water, about 200 yards off shore from the dock on Little Wapomeo Island. Tom had a bruise near his temple and fishing line was wrapped several times around his ankle. Due to the condition of the body, he was quickly buried at the Canoe Lake Cemetery, only to be moved several days later to the family plot at Leith, Ontario. Martin Blecher Sr. read the funeral service. Several days later an inquest into the death was held at the Blecher cabin. Subsequently it came to light that the night before Tom disappeared, Tom and Martin Jr. had apparently had a disagreement at a party at a neighbour's cabin. It was said that both left hot under the collar. This led to the speculation by local residents that Martin Jr. had more directly participated in the death of Tom Thomson than was previously thought. The evidence was only circumstantial, but these revelations added to suspicions that the Blechers were unsavory characters.

After Martin Sr.'s death in 1919, his wife Louisa assumed the Blecher lease. Martin Jr. eventually married and moved to the boathouse while his mother and sister lived in the main house. Louisa added a large "No Trespassing" sign, and another sign that gave notice: "$100 to be paid for information leading to the arrest of anyone damaging the property."[14] As the stories about the Blechers got passed down through the decades, the property became known to the kids on the lake as the "Ghost House." Many were told by their parents never to go near the place. According to Mary Margaret Armstrong Withey,

> "Sometimes the Blechers would be very friendly, and then
> a little later they wouldn't want anything to do with you.
> They would even push you off their property."[15]

---

[14]Correspondence in the Ministry lease archives.
[15]Correspondence in the Ministry lease archives.

Once Mrs. Blecher chased after Mark Robinson, the local park ranger, with her broom because he reminded her that she needed to fly the American flag below not above the Union Jack on her flag pole.[16] The locals were convinced that the Blechers sat there with binoculars watching the lake and all that passed by. There is of course no proof of this and in fact the "peeping tom" was likely a photographer neighbour across the way who loved to take pictures from his dock using his telephoto lens.

Martin Jr. seemed to enjoy puttering around the lake, though according to some not always with enough regard for those in canoes. His boat, called "Putt-Putt," would be heard going past Mowat every morning at dawn to Canoe Lake Station to meet the train, a common entertainment for many locals. Louisa gained her own notoriety as a result of a mistake in judgement that began just after Martin Sr.'s death. For whatever reasons, she applied for and was given permission to build a fence around her property. Her apparent objective was to keep Mowat Lodge tourists from wandering onto her property and bothering her. Later the fence was extended to include several neighbouring parcels as well. But the real uproar didn't begin until 1925. That year, Louisa built a boathouse by the shore and extended her fence to encompass two acres of land to the south of this part of the lake.[17] It prevented anyone from landing on the shore and walking up to the access road that ran behind all of the buildings on that side of town. This was considered a great inconvenience to a large number of tourists and leaseholders who frequented the lake. A group of them signed a petition and sent it to the Department advising,

> "That they wished that the lakefront landing and use of
> the road leading from it not be disturbed. We have made
> improvements to those facilities and its free use is of many
> years standing."[18]

---

[16]Mark Robinson 1917 Diary, Trent University Archives.

[17] The details of this story come from correspondence in the Ministry lease archives.

[18] Correspondence in the Ministry lease archives.

When confronted by the Department, Louisa claimed to be shocked at the reaction in the community. She wrote through her lawyers that the fence,

> "Only housed that land, which is part of my lease. I will be more than willing to show any officials the situation, explain matters and right any wrong that had been committed."[19]

A park ranger, W. L. Lewis, was sent to investigate. His inspection report filed later that year indicated that her boathouse was more than halfway outside the southern most boundary of her lot and was sitting directly on the landing spot. The Department lawyers wrote,

> "Mrs. Blecher should well consider whether she should in the interests of amity and good feeling, permit her neighbours and visitors to the lake to continue to use the landing and the road as in the past."[20]

There are also some notes that suggest that eventually the land in front of the new Mowat Lodge, built in 1921, became the new lakefront landing site (called Fraser's Landing). As was reported by Mr. Lewis,

> "At present the public land in front of Mowat Lodge bears a lot of traffic by cottagers and those stopping at the two large camps on Canoe Lake. It leaves the front yard of the hotel littered with hay and other litter and is not very desirable from the viewpoint of a private leaseholder. A landing could be made to the south of the Blecher lot but at considerable expense for stone and earth filling. There is a road leading up from that point which joins another road leading to Canoe Lake Station, therefore landing at this point could be a convenience to quite a lot of summer guests at the lake."[21]

There is no mention in the Department lease archives of exactly how the matter got finally resolved. But the issue apparently died, as there is no

---

[19] Ibid.
[20] Ibid.
[21] Ibid.

record of Mrs. Blecher being asked to remove her fence or move the boat-house. It may have been that as the town of Mowat decreased in size and influence, interest in the area's use as a lake access point diminished. However, it did add to the reputation of the Blechers as being "difficult" and they became quite estranged from the community.

Louisa apparently kept a low profile on the Canoe Lake scene until 1933 when she wrote a formal request to the Department for an investigation into the "deplorable condition of a garbage dump maintained by the camps on the west shore."[22] Though the arrival of Camp Wapomeo for Girls was a welcome addition to the Canoe Lake community, the resulting accumulation of garbage was not. There are no records available to explain how it came about but the east shore of the entrance to Whiskey Jack Creek became the site of the Camp Wapomeo dump. As a result of Louisa's inquiry, two park rangers came out to investigate but no report of any consequence was forthcoming. By 1935, Louisa was mad and undertook on her own to have a detailed water analysis done. The Ontario Department of Health advised her that all the water around the entry to the creek was very contaminated. In 1936 Louisa again wrote to advise that another dump had been started just south of the existing one. This time it was in the form of a floating raft with the contents partly in the water. This raft was destroyed by fire (one assumes lit by the camp maintenance staff) but another dump was then started 400 feet south of the remains of the original floating raft. As Louisa so eloquently stated herself,

> "One cannot believe that civilized people can be so filthy as to permit the condition to exist, which I observed this morning. Directly on the shoreline was a large pile of excrement and toilet paper dumped there from toilet cans along with garbage, tin cans, mattresses etc. There is seepage from the litter into the water even with the water level being some 3 feet below normal. I cannot be assured of health with such filthy conditions existing so close to my home."[23]

---

[22]Ibid.
[23]Ibid.

From a 21st century environmental perspective, it's difficult to imagine that such conditions were ever allowed to exist in Algonquin Park. Alas, it wasn't until the 1970s that human impact on the environment became well understood. However, by the 1940s, other residents echoed Louisa's complaints and eventually the dump was closed in the late 1940s. Today there is little evidence that the dump ever existed. All garbage is now trucked out of the park, or to a special landfill in the Park off Highway 60.

In the early spring of 1938, Martin Blecher Jr. died of a heart attack and his American second wife, Carolyn, was forced to return to the U.S. because she was not a Canadian citizen. Not long before, Martin Jr. had considered taking out his own lease on Smoke Lake but died before final arrangements could be made. One resident recalls coming up that spring and finding a hearse at the Canoe Lake landing. Looking up the lake he saw a couple of men with lanterns pulling a sled that he found out later bore the body of Martin Blecher Jr. That eerie image stuck with him for decades. Some time after the funeral, Louisa reported that a number of Martin's personal belongings had been stolen including a Fairbanks lathe, a drill press, a grinder, a hacksaw and various pulleys and hefts. These tools had been packed away for safe keeping in a cedar chest and locked in the boathouse. A $100 reward was offered, and as Louisa wrote,

> "Many persons knew of these tools and were anxious to obtain them for their personal use, or act as agents in obtaining them for others."[24]

None of his tools were ever found or returned but the fuss that Louisa raised with the Department solidified her reputation as being odd, reclusive, secretive and difficult. Louisa died in 1944 and the Blecher lease was passed on to her daughter Bessie, who died in 1951. Eventually the Blecher lease was sold to one of the Armstrong children who kept it until 1997, when it was sold to its current owners. By then the main house was pretty rundown. It was torn down in the fall of 1998 and a new cabin rebuilt on the site.

We will never really know what the Blecher women were like. There are few pictures, no diaries, no interview notes, and no memoirs that have been found. Louisa's concerns about the environment were real, though it

---

[24]Ibid.

would take another 30 years before there would be enough of a change in societal thinking to affect the management of Algonquin Park. It is nice to think that she might have been one of the early environmental activists.

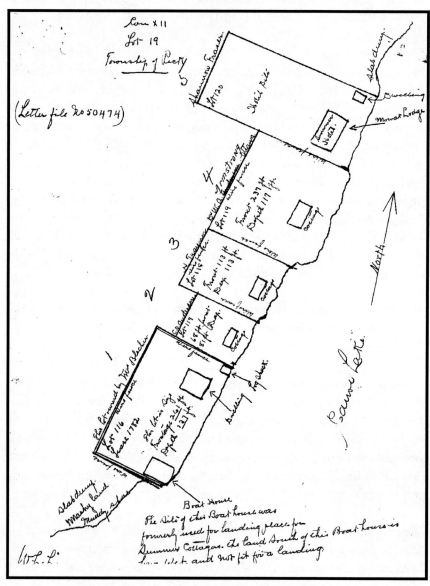

Hand Drawn Map of Mowat Leases Found in Lewis Report 1919—
MNR Lease Archives

Blecher Cabin, 1966—APMA #7105 MNR

Deer Grazing on Chip Yard with White Blecher House in the Background circa 1910s—
APMA #0072 Jack Wilkinson

Jennie Armstrong

Baggage Chute at Canoe Lake Station
Down to Potter Creek (known then as
Corkscrew Creek), 1959—APMA #1473 MNR

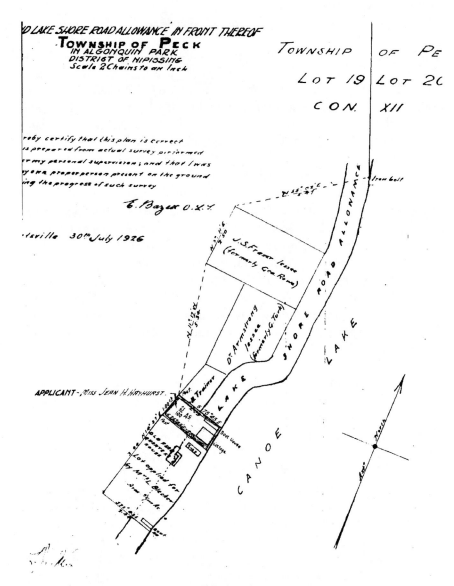

Survey of Mowat Lease Sites, 1926—MNR Lease Archives

Jennie Armstrong
(Recollections by Mary Margaret Armstrong Withey)

Though they didn't arrive on Canoe Lake until 1920, another family, the Armstrongs, faced many of the same challenges as the Piries in getting to Canoe Lake. It is not known what brought him to Canoe Lake, but Dr. W. Armstrong, a dentist from Ottawa, bought a land parcel from Reverend George Turk. This land was located just south of the site that a year later became the second Mowat Lodge. Every summer Dr. Armstrong, his wife Jennie and their six children would journey there from Ottawa. The oldest Armstrong brothers would walk through to the cottage along the road from Canoe Lake Station, pick up their big freight canoe and paddle back to the station to meet the rest of the family. A summer's worth of belongings and supplies would be loaded and ferried back to the cottage. Like Jean Pirie, Jennie Armstrong must have loved the Park or she wouldn't have been willing to stay up there alone all summer long with six kids, no electricity, no running water, a woodstove for heat and cooking, and only coal oil lanterns and candles for light. Often there would also be a full house of relatives and friends who would come with their families to visit. Sometimes there were so many visitors that the entire cabin looked like one giant dormitory.

Dr. Armstrong would appear every second or third weekend and loved taking the family on overnight canoe trips. Everyone in the family, even the girls, learned to expertly paddle a canoe, light a fire, set up a tent and chop wood with an axe. Robert, the oldest brother, used to occasionally guide for the local hotels. Like the Piries, food supplies were ordered from Eaton's, although occasionally they were able to buy some meat through one of the local hotels. The kids fished a lot and stuffed themselves on raspberries and blueberries when they were in season. The big excitement on Saturday night was to meet the train at Canoe Lake Station and ride down to Joe Lake Station. There the kids would get an ice cream cone and checkout the local social scene. Sometimes there would be a square dance attended by workers from the mill and visitors lodged at local guest houses and hotels. For the workers from the mill, many of whom were Polish from Barry's Bay, dancing was serious business. One set of visitors, who later became leaseholders, heading out on a canoe trip, recalled arriving on the late train and having a difficult nights sleep on the bare floor in the Joe Lake Station waiting room. Next door the locals were square dancing up a storm. The stomping of their heavy-booted feet on the loose floorboards caused the whole building to bounce up an down.

By the early 1930s, the Canadian National Railway, which had acquired the Grand Trunk Railway, was running only three passenger trains into the Park. Incoming trains would arrive on Tuesdays, Thursdays and Saturdays and departing trains would leave on Mondays, Wednesdays and Fridays. Unfortunately, as the main trestle bridge near Cache Lake was no longer structurally sound, the trains running from the east only went as far as Algonquin Park Station. At that time the family would come in by train from Ottawa to Whitney and then take a regular authorized jitney speeder service from Whitney to Cache Lake operated by Henry Bowers of Whitney. They had to arrange to arrive in time to get the morning westbound train from Cache Lake to Canoe Lake. As the Park superintendent said at the time,

> "From Algonquin Park east there is no rail passenger service past Cache Lake, nor are we permitted to carry anyone on our cars except in emergencies and then only on the order of the railway superintendent. Work has started on the highway east of here and perhaps the road will be passable to Canoe Lake by the fall of 1935."[25]

Nevertheless, though getting there was inconvenient and likely very stressful, the family persevered. Once Highway 60 opened travel was somewhat simpler, though likely a bit more dangerous. According to one Canoe Lake resident, in 1936 it took nine hours to complete the 190-mile journey from Ottawa to Canoe Lake. The last 85 miles between Golden Lake and Canoe Lake was a single lane road negotiated at an average speed of 20 mph. Travelers were constantly afraid that they might meet another vehicle coming the other way as they approached the crests of hills. It was also possible to take the morning train from Ottawa and arrive at Barry's Bay at noon. A taxi driver could be found to drive the visitor the rest of the way to Canoe Lake for about $10, a fortune in those days.[26]

---

[25]According to a 1934 note from the Park superintendent, in the Ministry lease archives.
[26]Memories provided by Hank Laurier, Canoe Lake resident.

Canoe Lake Station with Arriving GTR Passenger Train, 1915—
APMA #0028 Jack Wilkinson

Mowat Lodge after 1920, Original Armstrong Cabin Above Arrow—
APMA #222 Aubrey Dunne

Highway 60 Under Construction, 1934—
APMA #1268 J. Leech-Porter

Highway 60 Road Surface, 1936—
APMA #2394 Anne Prewitt

Chapter 2
The Business Women

The Business Women

I run my own consulting business helping high technology companies improve their sales effectiveness. A few years ago I made a commitment to myself and my kids to spend at least a month every year at Canoe Lake. I've learned the hard way that it's a huge mistake to tell that to my clients as they tend to forget when I said I'd return. The first few times I left the country I saw a terrible drop-off in my business, which took months to rebuild. So I've decided to wire the cabin for the Internet age and make Canoe Lake my Canadian branch office. First arrangements needed to be made for the phone company to convert from analog to digital service, i.e., touch-tone rather than rotary dialing. This enabled me to attach answering machines and connect laptop computers. Until the early 1980s we had a party line telephone shared with several neighbours. We each had different ring combinations. Ours was "two longs," which made racing up from the dock quite frustrating if one was half way up the hill and the tone turned out to be "one long - one short." Sometimes as kids we would listen in on our neighbours' conversations, which always sounded like it would be much more exciting than it really was. Most adult conversations it turned out were quite boring – at least to a kid.

The next challenge that I have is to rewire the cottage phone lines so that I can keep my laptop tucked away in the corner of the room rather than out in the middle of the kitchen near the phone jack. I reminisce of the days when I could have called Bell Canada and she'd have sent out a repairman to get the job done. Today, self-service is the name of the game. To hire someone to do it would cost a fortune and there'd be no guarantee that the work would get done during the few weeks that I am in residence. As I sort out the black, yellow, green and orange wires and connect the new phone lines. I remember the summer when a Bell Canada repairman did appear out of the forest like a mirage. It turned out that unbeknownst to us, he'd arrived by boat on the other side of the ridge to fix the line at a neighbour's cabin. He had made arrangements to be picked up that afternoon from our dock after he traced the line to make sure there were no other breaks in it. No one told us and his sudden appearance out of the forest, briefcase in hand, scared us half to death.

Once the wiring is sorted out I then have to figure out how to configure the laptop interfaces so that it can properly connect to the local Internet access hub, which isn't really local at all. The closest connection to my supposedly global ISP is still a 165-mile long distance call to Toronto. Eventually I am able to make the connections work, but the transmission speed is very slow. It takes ages to download e-mail messages and searching the Internet, though doable, is very tedious. I wonder in a moment of fantasy if high-speed satellite or wireless connections are available yet. In general the system works though I am not very productive. I check voice mail everyday and e-mail every few days and "business" for the most part continues on. None of my clients realize that I am sitting by a lake 35 miles from the closest town and 165 miles north of the closest major airport. Occasionally someone has a call identifier service and can't recognize the area code and asks where I am. Then I am found out. The only catch is if a customer needs to see me in person. Then things gets a little tricky. Last August I discovered another problem when it got quite cold one night. Computers don't like 40-degree weather and it takes quite some time to warm them up by the fire or in the sunshine, so that they will work again. Though we think of Canoe Lake now as a respite from work, as the Portage Store and Arowhon Pines Resort are the only businesses nearby, my experience has shown me that this is not always the case. The truth is that I am only one in a long line of hardworking women who have run businesses on Canoe Lake.

The kids and I decide to go on a hike north up Potter Creek to see if we can find any remains of these businesses. We first take the boat up to the Joe Lake Dam and cross the portage on foot. On the far side, we walk up past the canoe landing spot and find a small path that works its way north. It spills out at the railway bridge where Joe Lake proper opens up. I stand on the bridge and imagine what it must have looked like when Molly Colson was here. On the shore right in front of me is where the Colson dock and outfitting store once sat. Now it is thick forest. Up on the hill above us is where the Algonquin Hotel once stood in its majesty. Just down the shore was George Rowe's cabin. Now, though, the forest has reclaimed this world. I turn around and look in the other direction. There are no signs that this is about the location of Mark Robinson's cabin. Mark lived and worked around these shores for nearly 40 years. Apparently at one time Department regulations prohibited or at least disapproved of families of Park rangers living with them. Mark would travel to visit his family in Barrie several times a year. It was only in later years that the family would come to the Park to visit him for a few weeks during the summer. He'd faithfully mail his wife his paycheque each month and wrote letters weekly. What a lonely life it must have been for both of them.

We walk back along the old railroad bed that is now a dirt road and turn south at a junction that is approximately where Canoe Lake Station must have once stood. We sit down on an old stump and survey the scene while eating our sandwiches. Nothing remains of the old baggage chute that used to connect this spot to the creek below. After we finish our lunch we follow the road south parallel to Potter's Creek. It winds its way behind the few cottages that remain. Just before the turn-off to the cemetery we stop and look out over what must have been the old chip yard. Today it's all open water. Well-preserved wooden planks, manufactured by the long-defunct Canoe Lake Mills, are submerged in 10 feet or so of water and covered with sediment and only visible from directly above in a canoe when the sun shines at the right angle. Directly south of us is the old mill foundation. There is no sign of Mowat Lodge or the cabin by the water that once graced this spot. As I gaze, my mind drifts again. An image of Mowat Lodge rises from the mists around me. I can see Annie coming from the barn carrying two pails of milk with a few fresh eggs tucked in her apron pocket. The verandah is awash with guests and guides chattering in the sunlight. Down by the shore, a little distance away, a solitary painter stands contemplating his canvas, brush in hand. The image fades and we continue on our way up the hill to the cemetery to see how it has fared over the winter.

Annie Fraser

Annie Fraser (center) with husband, Shannon (right)
and a Friend at Smoke Lake—APMA #4046 Mary Northway

Annie Fraser – Mowat Lodge Proprietress

In 1907 Annie Fraser and her husband Shannon moved to the small town of Mowat on the northwest shores of Canoe Lake. Shannon Fraser had been appointed to supervise the settling and dismantling of the then bankrupt Canoe Lake Mills. In trying to piece together what had happened, Annie discovered that the unraveling of the fortunes of the Gilmour Brothers had begun with their disastrous 1896 attempt to haul logs from Algonquin Park to Trenton.[27] The mission of Canoe Lake Mills was to prepare "deals," wooden planks 3 to 4 inches thick that were to be shipped to specialty mills to be cut into the sizes needed to build houses and furniture. Gilmour was granted a 10-year "license of occupation" for $40 per year, covering 326 acres west and a short way south of Potter Creek near the Gilmour logging camp. The tote road from Tea Lake was extended north and a huge boiler was hauled up from the Dorset pump house. Nine teams of horses were used to pull the boiler on birch rollers that wore out almost as fast as the men could cut them. The construction workers worked three shifts per day to get the mill in operation in time for the spring log drive of 1897. Canoe Lake was apparently at the time a complete mass of floating logs. The official conditions of granting such a license included:

- The licensees shall keep the said premises clean and in good sanitary condition, free from filth, rubbish or debris.

- The licensees shall properly survey and layout in lots and trees ... on which it is proposed to erect workmen's houses . . . all dwellings . . . shall be of good construction . . . and when made of boards they shall be painted or whitewashed.

- The licensees shall pay one-half the salary of a Park Ranger whose duty it shall be, amongst, other things, to see that no such violations occurs.[28]

Gilmour must have been aware that this location was near the new Ottawa, Arnprior and Parry Sound railway line then being built by J. R. Booth. The Ottawa, Arnprior and Parry Sound railway officially opened in early

---

[27] Details as to this endeavour can be found in *Canoe Lake and the Tom Thomson Mystery*, by S. Bernard Shaw, 1995.

[28] Excerpted from *Early Days in Algonquin Park*.

1897 and ran from Depot Harbour on Georgian Bay to Arnprior and traveled 36 miles through Algonquin Park. Canoe Lake Station was established at the north end of Potter Creek and Joe Lake Station a little to the east on Joe Lake. It had a water tank, pump house and numerous sidings. As the creek was a lower elevation than the railway station, a baggage chute was built to move luggage from the train down to water's edge. Like logs on a flume, the baggage would fly down the hill to the dock and be loaded into boats or canoes waiting at creekside. It's been said that in the early 1900s, trains would pass every 20 minutes carrying grain from the west among other valuable cargo. Mrs. Ratan, the railway section boss's wife, was the first station mistress. She tried to keep the place clean and in a fit of pique one day posted a sign in the station waiting room:

"Gentlemen WILL not,
Ladies DO not,
Others MUST not
Spit on the floor."[29]

Soon after the new railway opened, a 2.4-kilometer rail spur called the "Gilmour Spur" was built from the main line at Canoe Lake station to the new mill. A switching station was erected in an open area of sand and gravel called Sim's Pit, a mile east of Joe Lake Station. Later, Sim's Pit served as a layover spot for an extra railway crew posted during World War I to provide lookouts against train sabotage. In 1903 J. R. Booth sold the Ottawa, Arnprior and Parry Sound Railway to the Grand Trunk Railway System. In 1923 Grand Trunk itself was purchased by the Canadian National Railway, which went through the northern part of the park at Brent and Kiosk.

For Annie it was hard to believe that the little town of Mowat with its 205 residents had at one time been home to more than 700 people clustered around the Gilmour mill and the railway line.[30] A post office was established in 1897 with E. T. Marsh as the first postmaster. At that time, Mowat had a hospital, a boarding house, stables for 50 teams of horses, a large warehouse, cookhouse, various storehouses, farm buildings, shacks and a small cemetery up on a knoll northwest of town. The cemetery's only

---

[29] *Early Days in Algonquin Park*, pg. 20-21.
[30] Mowat named after the then-Ontario Premier, Oliver Mowat.

occupant for many years was James Watson, who had died in 1897 in a mill accident. His fellow workers engraved the following inscription:

"Remember Comrades (when passing by), As you are now, so once was I. As I am now so you shall be, Prepare thyself to follow me."[31]

Later, in 1915, a black throat diphtheria epidemic took the life of 8-year-old Alexander Hayhurst who was also then buried there. But it wasn't until the temporary interment of Tom Thomson in 1917, marked today by a small white cross, that the cemetery got its air of mystery and intrigue.

Because there were so many children, the Gilmour employees asked for a school. A grant of $100 was received from the Ontario Department of Education to do so. With additional contributions from parents, a teacher was hired at a $200 annual salary and a schoolhouse was built just off the road that joined Canoe Lake Station to Mowat. Unfortunately, after the area was reforested in the 1960s, all of the landmarks that might have indicated where the school was located disappeared. The best source is a hand-drawn map, published in 2000, based on the recollections of Eleanor Mooney Wright.[32]

In 1898 prices for white pine dropped, so the Gilmours decided to stockpile most of the top grade lumber. In order to create a large enough storage area, sawdust, pine slabs and inferior logs were dumped into the lake along side of the mill until it made a solid surface. This became known as the "chip yard." By 1900 the whole logging scheme and Canoe Lake Mills went bankrupt. The Gilmours boarded up their residences on the island and abandoned the area by 1901. Little effort was made to clean up the mess or return the area to its original condition as required in the "license of occupation." In 1906, the Gilmour receivers convinced the Ontario Government to extend the Gilmour "license of occupation" for another five years to facilitate a more complete liquidation of the assets. During these years, many of the better buildings, including the hospital, boarding house and kitchen, and various outbuildings were sold to arriving

---

[31]In 1927, the boys from Ahmek held a minstrel show and added the following lines to the James Watson's headstone: **"To follow you I's not content, Until I know which way you went."**
[32]Wright, H.E. Mooney, *Joe Lake: Reminiscences of an Algonquin Park Ranger's Daughter*, HEW Enterprises, Eganville, 1999 pgs. x/xi.

leaseholders and moved to their lease sites. The rail spur was dismantled and the rails sold to Colonel J. J. Gartshore, head of General Steel Wares, who claimed that he had purchased more than 11 miles of steel.

The Frasers spent their first six years at Mowat leasing a 1.72-acre site that included the old hospital up on a hill above the old mill site. In 1913 they decided that the tourist trade had some promise. They sold the hospital lease site and acquired a lease that included the old mill-hand kitchen and boarding house. This they turned into Camp Mowat. A Mr. R. P. Little claimed to have been the first guest in the fall of 1913. The camp, later renamed Mowat Lodge was,

> "An unprepossessing two-story, white-washed, wooden struc-
> ture with a veranda across the front. Set on rising ground some
> distance from the water it faced the old mill yard, a treeless,
> desolate area of thirty acres or more covered with pine slabs and
> sawdust. Some abandoned buildings from former days were still
> standing (a horse barn, a storehouse etc.) and by the lakeshore
> were the ruins of the old mill."[33]

Pictures of Annie show her to be a smallish, slightly stout woman with wavy brown hair and kindly eyes. According to every story, she was industrious and very hardworking. She kept her own cows and chickens, which supplied the hotel with fresh milk and eggs. At first Mowat Lodge catered to campers visiting Canoe Lake and advertised their ability to provide meals at the lodge, supplies and mail for those who wished to camp at one of the lake's many campsites. Later they started supplying boxed lunches and would deliver them around the lake to those folks camping or picnicking at various spots.[34] They also advertised the medicinal value of fresh air and a wilderness environment, which attracted people recovering from lung-related illnesses who would come and stay for long periods of time.

Mowat Lodge was an immediate financial success. It was considered third place in quality after the Highland Inn and the Algonquin Hotel. This was no doubt due to its reasonable rates, very rustic and casual atmosphere and Annie's excellent cooking. There were occasionally some complaints about its inadequate heating and makeshift furnishings, but nature provided a form of compensation:

---

[33] Addison, O., with Elizabeth Harwood, *Tom Thomson—The Algonquin Years*, Ryerson Press, Toronto, 1969, pg. 13.
[34] *Early Days in Algonquin Park*, pg. 80.

"Wildlife was plentiful in the surrounding area. Deer would wander across the chip yard and beaver swam in the bay nearby."[35]

However, as renowned artist and frequent Canoe Lake visitor and later a member of the 'Group of Seven' A.Y. Jackson put it in 1914,

"The area around Canoe Lake at the time was a ragged piece of Nature, hacked up many years ago by a lumber company that went broke. It was fire-swept, damned by both man and beaver and overrun with wolves."[36]

Shannon Fraser, known as Shan, was tall with bright red curly hair and freckles. He was well spoken, good-natured, a charismatic talker and showman, full of great ideas. He loved to be the center of attention, though some locals thought he was lazy. For them, his outgoing behaviour was an excuse he made to make Annie and his old mother do all of the work. He never liked to be seen in anything other than a blue suit, shirt, tie and fedora, but apparently wasn't much of a businessman. He had a bad habit of going off and doing whatever he wanted even though Annie and others would disagree. One year, to Annie's horror, he went ahead and advertised a nonexistent open fireplace in the lobby. Annie was adamant that they couldn't afford to build it, but the brochure was already being printed, so she reluctantly agreed. Another time he decided that visitors disembarking the train needed to be greeted properly, so he bought a horse-drawn coach that became known as "The Hearse" from an undertaker. He would meet the train each day and drive people down to the lodge or to wherever they wanted to go. One year he was given an unofficial title as the "Mayor of Mowat."

After 1914 Mowat Lodge became somewhat of an artists' haunt due to the influence of Tom Thomson and his fellow artists who would follow him to the Park and paint. As was suggested in "The Algonquin Story," the first written history of Algonquin Park,

"Their paintings had to dry before being packed, so Mowat Lodge would overflow with all of these latest sketches. Guests and artists alike would share in friendly criticisms and unstinting praise of most recent experiments."[37]

---

[35] *Tom Thomson—The Algonquin Years*, pg. 14
[36] Meehan, B. (curator), Millard, L. (text), *Algonquin Memories—Tom Thomson in Alogonquin Park*, Exhibition for the Algonquin Gallery in Algonquin Park, 1998, opposite Plate #3.
[37] Saunders, A., *The Algonquin Story*, Ontario Department of Lands and Forests, Toronto, 1946, pg. 169.

Though nothing is known today as to the cause, the original Mowat Lodge was destroyed by fire in November of 1920. There is some speculation by locals that the cause was a knocked-over coal oil lantern or sparks from the fireplace. Annie and her daughter Mildred were away at the time and little was salvaged except some livestock and fowl. The Frasers abandoned the site and moved to a little cottage, bought from George Rowe down by the lake.[38] They took out a lease for the property next to the old mill foundation and had Mowat Lodge re-built. The old Mowat Lodge site reverted to the crown in 1923 and later was leased by various leaseholders. Today all that remains is an oil drum that hides the remains of the well, a few collapsed outbuildings and a cabin built by a leaseholder on the site in the late 1940s.

Like the original, the new Mowat Lodge was an immediate success and survived until late 1930 or early 1931 when it and the Frasers' little cottage burned to the ground. The exact date has always been a mystery as a search of both the Huntsville Forester and the Superintendents Reports (which usually reported on every Park activity) for 1930 and 1931 made no mention of Mowat Lodge's demise. This time Shan and Annie gave up, moved to Kearney and then later to Huntsville. In 1931, the charred ruins reverted to the crown. Annie Fraser disappeared from the Canoe Lake history books until 1977 when Roy MacGregor interviewed Daphne Crombie. It seems that Crombie and her war veteran husband, Robert, had been at Canoe Lake, staying at Mowat Lodge druing the spring and summer of 1917. She had met Tom Thomson and become friends with Annie Fraser. According to Crombie, there had been a party at George Rowe's cabin with lots of drinking, at which Tom had gotten into an argument with Shannon over some money that was owed him. There was a fistfight and Tom had fallen against the fire grate, receiving the mysterious temple wound. In a panic, Fraser roused Annie and forced her to help him dispose of the body in the lake by weighing it down with stones tied with fishing line. Though plausible, there is some disagreement as to when such an altercation might have happened. Crombie thought it had taken place the night before Thomson died on July 7, 1917. But he was apparently seen on the morning of July 8th by both Mark Robinson, the local ranger, and Shannon Fraser. Roy MacGregor suggests that maybe the altercation took place after Tom returned from his fishing trip as his canoe wasn't reported missing until July 9th, and not found until the following day, July 10. The truth may have been that Shannon Fraser had argued with Tom not at a party, but

---

[38]For more insight into the adventures of George Rowe, please see the story of Molly Cox Colson.

after Tom's return to Mowat Lodge. Bernard Shaw refuted this assertion in his 1995 book, but an aura of mystery now surrounds this woman and her husband, who likely knew a lot more than was ever indicated about the events that took place that July on Canoe Lake.

Annie Fraser in Front of Fireplace at Mowat Lodge, 1922—APMA #1016 MNR

Shannon Fraser with "The Hearse"— APMA #3010 Alex Edmison

(Left to right) Shan Fraser and Mrs. Fraser, Mrs. Edwin Thomas & Rose Thomas—APMA #48 Jack Wilkinson

New Mowat Lodge, 1922 Before Addition— APMA #1809 W.B. Tilden

View of Canoe Lake from Cemetery likely in 1920s—
APMA #6932 Adele Ebbs Collection

Original Mowat Lodge before 1920—
APMA #6927 Adele Ebbs Collection

Molly Cox Colson

Ed and Molly Colson at the Highland Inn,
circa 1910s—APMA #2891 Mary Colson Clare

Molly Cox Colson

Another anchor for the Canoe Lake community for most of the first half of the 20th century was Molly Cox Colson. She first came to Algonquin Park in May 1900 to visit with her good friends Dr. and Mrs. William Bell at Cache Lake. Dr. Bell had just joined the Algonquin Park ranger staff and was in the process of drafting the first Algonquin Park canoe route map. Molly was a nurse from Ottawa and her doctors said she needed a well-deserved rest. She liked the Park enough that she decided to stay on. Her first job was as the housekeeper at the park rangers' boarding house at Cache Lake. She had a strong personality and soon had everyone under her thumb. As the superintendent of the Park at the time said,

> "The rangers had never been so well looked after as they were under Miss Cox's direction."[39]

She and Mrs. Bell used to startle other women by abandoning periodically their long flowing skirts for breeches, which were much more comfortable and much less cumbersome. Of occasional nuisance was the resident cow, which provided fresh milk for all of the ranger staff and families. It needed a constant supply of fresh grasses that were found along the railway track. The rangers hated the job of cutting grass for the cow even though they enjoyed the benefits of its presence. Later Molly also managed a tent city, which housed overflow Highland Inn guests.

Molly made the most of her nursing skills. She was a wonderful healer and became the local mid-wife, prenatal counselor, setter of broken bones and even pulled teeth on occasion. As there wasn't a doctor nearby, she would always make house calls when anyone was sick, even in winter. She gained local fame when she walked more than a mile from the Algonquin Hotel on Joe Lake to the Farley house on Potter Creek using two canes. There she promptly delivered one of the Farley daughters who was arriving prematurely. In another incident, a man at a local lumbering camp had fractured his leg and needed a splint before he could be moved. Molly set the bone and bound the leg using a splint that her husband, Ed, made out of a piece of board. The man was taken to the doctor at Whitney, who found that he didn't need to reset the leg at all—it had been set perfectly.

---

[39] *The Algonquin Story*, pg. 125.

An incident that illustrates the depth of Molly's compassion involved the pregnant wife of one of the railroad section men. She had come into labour early and the doctor was in bed with the flu, so Molly was the only alternative. The woman's husband hightailed it from their home in Rock Lake to Molly for help. In the midst of a terrible wind and lightning storm, Molly and the husband raced to the woman's aid in Rock Lake on a six-wheeled, gas-powered railroad "speeder" handcart. Unfortunately the baby had died and the woman was in terrible shape. Molly stayed there for four days nursing her back to health. According to some in the district at the time,

> "Molly did everything for her neighbours but marry them and bury them and her husband could do those two things if needed."[40]

Once Molly herself had to be rushed out of the Park because she had a bowel obstruction of some kind. By the time they got her to the hospital, on a gas-driven handcar that resided at Canoe Lake Station, she was fine. All the jiggling and bouncing on the handcar had dislodged the obstruction.

Ed Colson first came to the Park from Guelph as a ranger in 1905. He was a quiet man and somewhat withdrawn but he and Molly fell in love and got married in 1907. In 1908 they both were hired to manage the Highland Inn, which had recently been built by the Grand Trunk Railway. The Highland Inn boasted of indoor washrooms, hot and cold running water, fine meals as well as complete canoe tripping guide and outfitting services.

> "It was a far cry from roughing it in the bush. Guests were dressed impeccably by today's standards and gathered for formal dining in the main lodge. Many of the locals used to comment that if you went to the Highland Inn you had to be a big shot."[41]

In 1917 Ed and Molly Colson decided to buy the Algonquin Hotel at Joe Lake Station and left the Highland Inn. Lawrence Merrill from Rochester, New York, had built the Algonquin Hotel in 1908, the same year as the Highland Inn.[42] It was located partway up a hill, set back from the railway

---

[40] *The Algonquin Story*, pg. 127.

[41] Interviews with Mary Colson Clare, by Don Standfield in 1992, found in the Ministry Archives, and with the author in 1999.

[42] Most Algonquin Park narratives refer to him as Tom Merrill, but Mark Robinson in his diaries refers to him as Lawrence Merrill several times.

line that crossed the south end of Joe Lake, just north of the dam and southwest of the Joe Lake Station. It had a lovely view out across Joe Lake.

The Algonquin Hotel was considered by most to be a bit more rustic than the Highland Inn. The outside was made of custom cut wood slabs, and by and large its patrons tended to like to rough it a bit. Guests would usually come for a month and spend time picnicking, hiking, swimming or fishing on the lake or in the local area. Over time it became a favourite place to launch fishing trips into the interior of the Park. Often the women would gather on the veranda to talk, crochet, knit, play cards or go for walks around the property, while the men went on fishing expeditions. There were always a few women who would join their husbands on these trips, but most liked the hotel and its environment and were especially happy when their husbands went off for a few days and left them to themselves.

According to Ed Colson's niece, Mary Colson Clare, the hotel had about 20 rooms, two big screened-in porches and three bathrooms shared by all the guests.[43] There were various wood stoves that would be lit when it got cool in early spring or late fall. Each bedroom was equipped with a nice wash stand with pitcher, oil lamps for late night reading, iron or wooden beds, and nice wooden dressers. In the kitchen was a big wood-burning range that was unbearably hot for summer cooking, but a great generator of heat in the chill of spring and fall. The hotel charged $18 to $22 a week for the most expensive rooms, including all meals. One person's job for the whole season was to wash and iron all the hotel linens using a propane washing machine and a great big electric ironing machine. After a long stint at the Highland Inn, Lizzie Dennison, granddaughter of Captain Dennison from Lake Opeongo, became the main cook. She would also help in the spring getting the hotel ready for the summer guests. In winter she would cook at a nearby lumber camp. All of the dishes were heavy china and the dining room would fit 50 or 60 people sitting on pressed back chairs at eight wooden tables covered with fresh linen tablecloths. In the early 1930s when the hotel was occupied during the winter, the dining room became a walk-in freezer for the supplies that were brought in every two weeks.

Next to the hotel, the Colsons established the Joe Lake Outfitting Store (known as the Colson Store by locals) to offer canoe tripping guides and

---

[43]Ed Colson's brother George's daughter.

49

outfitting. At the time, Algonquin Park was a favourite spot for camping and fishing. Few visitors would dare attempt a fishing trip without knowing how to manage a canoe, and if they weren't knowledgeable about survival in the woods, they looked to hire a guide. The guides all came from the surrounding area. Many would log or trap all winter and guide for the hotel all summer. It took awhile to get used to their wild appearance as backwoods bushwackers, but once you got to know them, the guides proved to be most interesting conversationalists. They didn't make much money, maybe $5 a day, but they all sure knew how to look after the guests in the bush. As Mary Colson Clare said,

> "It was most incongruous to see women from the hotel with washed skin and clean dresses chatting with these old-faced, leathery skinned guides who were constantly scratching their heads."[44]

According to local fishing guide and writer Ralph Bice, the Colson Store in its heyday was the best outfitting store in the Park. Ed brought in his sister Annie Colson, known as Aunt Annie by everyone, to run it. Though somewhat severe looking, Annie Colson was well loved by all. She had a difficult childhood as her mother had died when she was a teenager and it had become her responsibility to raise the family. She lived with her brother and Molly most of her life and had previously been in charge of the outfitting store at Highland Inn. Annie could:

> "Set up a list of supplies as well as most guides. People would call or write in their tripping orders before they came up. She would pack all their flour, rice and whatever else they wanted in cotton bags. The eggs were packed into pails and along with tents and blankets were packed into big packsacks. No one had sleeping bags in those days."[45]

Annie had her hands full looking after the customers as well as children from all over the area running around and getting in the way. All the kids

---

[44]Interviews with Mary Colson Clare by Don Standfield in 1992, and with the author in 1999.
[45]Bice, R., *Along the Trail with Ralph Bice in Algonquin Park*, Natural Heritage/Natural History Inc, Toronto, 1980, pg. 54.

knew that Annie had a weakness for children, so most were waiting for handouts that she would slip to them. She must have not minded too much as she would always let the children know in advance when the hotel ordered ice cream so that they could be the first to buy.[46]

The hotel was open from early May until the end of September. This all meant that Colson Outfitting Store was a busy and popular meeting place for guests, guides, leaseholders and staff from the children's camp. There was always some reason to stop by. Most wanted to get supplies at the Colson Store, talk to the guides or to Ed Colson or just generally hang around. According to Mary Colson Clare, the Colsons usually made enough money through the summer with the outfitting store and the hotel that they could survive during the winter. In the 1920s the hotel was supplied by freight trains with a little half-passenger car at the back that ran four times a day in summer and once a week in winter. Arriving from Toronto passengers had to disembark at Scotia Junction and wait for the next train to come through from Ottawa or from Parry Sound. Sometimes the engineers and conductors would let the local kids ride the trains down to Canoe Lake Station from Joe Lake Station.

Guiding tourists was an interesting profession and relatively lucrative for winter loggers or trappers. Most of the tourists were Americans since few Canadians at the time were interested in putting, as one local indicated, pleasure before financial security. Guides had to be approved and licensed at $2 a year by the Park superintendent upon the recommendation of an inspector or game warden. The 1909 regulations of licenses for fishing guides made them responsible for:

- Extinguishing any fires that may have been kindled by the party employing him as guide
- Advising the Department of any violations of fish and game laws within one month after such offence, giving the name and address of offender and other particulars as will lead to the conviction of the party or parties committing the offence. [47]

Guides who neglected or refused to comply with these regulations were subject to penalties including the cancellation of their license and a bar from employment as a guide for two years. The hotel had a special "guide

[46] *Early Days in Algonquin Park*, pg. 75.
[47] Notice found in Mark Robinson Diaries of 1909.

house" where the guides stayed for free when not on a trip. The hotels would provide all canoes, (rented out at $1 per day) tents, gear and food. Most guides usually needed to be booked some weeks in advance. They paid for their own meals (25 cents a meal) if not under contract. Otherwise the tourist party involved paid for all of the guides' meals. Until 1920 they earned about $2 per day and an extra 50 cents if they used their own canoe. After 1920 the rate increased to $4 per day and $1 extra if a guide used his own canoe. In the 1930s Highland Inn fishing trip fees were quoted at $55 per week, including a guide, all equipment and gear.[48]

Bill Stoqua, a member of the Golden Lake Indian Band and a major contributor to the early success of Camp Ahmek, was one of the guides who worked at the hotel. He would arrive in early spring to help open up the hotel and do many of the spring cleaning jobs that needed to be done. He would bring little moccasins that his mother made during the winter for the Colson nieces and nephews. He was a great paddler and his paddling technique became the basis for the Ahmek Stroke (or Indian stroke as it was sometimes called). Everyone learned how to paddle by watching Bill and the other guides such as George Rowe, Lawrie Dickson, Bill Hayhurst and later Omer Stringer. The guides were all very helpful and friendly, and enjoyed teaching everyone anything they could. Most would stay just for the summer, but a few guides stayed on well into October for fall fishing trips once the hotel was closed.

Molly Colson's reputation as a lifesaver took on a new aura in the spring of 1918. George Rowe and Lawrie Dickson, the two local handymen and part-time guides, who had found the body of Tom Thomson floating in the water near Little Wapomeo Island the previous summer, had become somewhat famous in the community as a result. Earlier in his life Rowe had been a prize-winning typesetter, who won first prize at the Chicago Worlds Fair in the early 1890s. He came to Mowat in the 1900s to help dismantle the Gilmour machinery and decided to stay. He didn't seem to have any relatives but had a nice neat appearance, was patient and efficient and knew how to talk to people. He was a fabulous fishing guide and made great efforts to help his fishing parties feel comfortable. Dickson, on the other hand was a mess. Like Rowe he had come to Mowat in the early 1900s and for a time worked for the Mickle and Dymont Lumber Company.

---

[48] *Early Days in Algonquin Park*, pg. 89.

Later he worked for Mowat Lodge and sometimes the Algonquin Hotel as both handyman and sometime guide. He apparently had a son who used to come and see him occasionally, but no mention was ever made of a wife.

George and Lawrie were friends and lived together on and off for several years in one of the old Gilmour shacks up on the hill near the old hospital building. According to "The Algonquin Story," this was the cabin that became immortalized in Tom Thomson's painting, entitled "The Artist's Hut." A tale told by one local suggested that upon occasion they had to share the same bed. If they had been drinking too much and one happened to roll over and disturb the other during the night, the resulting uproar could be heard by everyone in the community. Neighbours sometimes wondered if one of them was being murdered. To help solve the problem, friends apparently got a long cedar pole and chained it to the top and bottom of the bed directly down the middle. Woe to the man that crossed that divider.

In the spring of 1918 the ice had gone out early. George and Lawrie were paddling up Joe Creek on a stormy April night. According to Mark Robinson, there was "heavy rain and storm with a high wind from the south."[49] The canoe hit a deadhead and dumped. Lawrie landed on a stump with a sharp point that pierced his lung. George clung to another stump and started shouting. The Colsons were a good half-mile upstream at the Algonquin Hotel. Whether or not it was intuition, good hearing or just plain luck, Molly was convinced that she had heard someone yelling and cajoled Ed to go out into the storm and investigate. He reached the struggling men just in time and brought them both back to the hotel. George recovered, but Lawrie, after resting for several days at the hotel was rushed down to Toronto General Hospital where he died on May 4, 1918. George was so grateful to Molly for saving his life that he wanted her to have "power of attorney" over his affairs, so that he couldn't draw any money from his war pension without her signature. He later signed on as a guide at the hotel, leased a cabin near Joe Lake Dam and allegedly never drank again.

In 1920 the Colsons decided that they needed a break from Canoe Lake. They moved to Renfrew to run Renfrew House, a Temperance house built by a mining magnate by the name of O'Brien. Annie Colson went off to Alberta to run an orphanage and Ed's brother George and his wife Mary

---

[49]Mark Robinson Diaries, April 1918.

took over the day-to-day running of the Algonquin Hotel. This worked well until 1927 when, at the age of 51, George died suddenly. Ed and Molly then returned to Algonquin Park and resumed the management of the hotel. Life was now very busy as lumbering in the Potter Creek area had been revived in 1926. The Canoe Lake Lumber Company had taken over the Gilmour lumbering limits and built a sawmill at Potter Creek. Alfred Clark, also owner of wholesale lumber merchants A. E. Clark & Son of Toronto, was trying to make a go of cutting hardwood. Loggers cut logs in Smoke Lake area all winter and in the spring would tow these hardwood logs up from Smoke Lake to the sawmill on 36-foot long cribs made of cedar logs. They used a 50-foot tugboat powered by a 40 horse-power single-cylinder steam engine that was fueled by slabs from the mill. The log booms were anchored from the Mowat Lodge waterfront all the way up to the mill on Potter Creek. These efforts didn't last and after a few years the site was abandoned. In 1939, when Joe Omanique tried to make a go of it, he built a road extension out to Highway 60 and the trestle bridge across Potter Creek.

In 1931, Mary Colson Clare was asked to teach school for $800 per year at the Canoe Lake School, which she did for a couple of years. [50] Due to the Depression, Ed and Molly Colson were living in the Algonquin Hotel year round, and Mary stayed with them in the rooms above the kitchen at the back of the hotel. As previously indicated the school was located on Potter Creek between the trestle bridge and Canoe Lake Station. Mary would walk everyday along the railway track about half a mile from Joe Lake and then back through the bush to the school. There were eight pupils in eight grades. Every morning Everett Farley, the resident postmaster and handyman, would light a fire in the pot-bellied stove to warm up the schoolroom before the children arrived. There were double desks and a little organ. The students would come every day regardless of the weather or distance. In the winter the students would heat flat chunks of wood on the stove to put on the floor under their double desks to keep their feet warm. Everyone would walk home for lunch and then return for the afternoon. Occasionally in winter the school inspector would come to visit from North Bay by train. He would stay at the hotel in one of the three bedrooms at the back that were heated by a stove. He never complained about accommodations that were semi-warm at best, but did jump back on the train as soon as he could.

[50] Excerpted from interviews with Mary Colson Clare, by Don Standfield in 1992 and Gaye Clemson in 1999.

The school had a baby grand piano that came from the defunct "Camp of the Red Gods," now Camp Arowhon on Teepee Lake, and a little organ that was used for Sunday church services. Ed Colson was a lay reader for the Church of England and would hold church services and Sunday school every week when there was no qualified clergy around. In the winter, everyone in the area would snowshoe over to the school, sometimes pulling Molly on a sleigh. In the summer, services would be held at Camp Ahmek and everyone would walk or paddle over for the service. Molly would play a little pump organ or the piano at camp, sing hymns and read Bible stories. Sometimes on Sunday nights those living at the north end would come to the Algonquin Hotel for chocolate cake and hymn singing. Once a year a bishop would come up from Ottawa to baptize any children and give them communion with Ed and Molly often named the godparents. Most years the Colsons would organize some type of Christmas concert. All of the kids would rehearse little plays over at the mill dining hall with a couple of old sheets for a backdrop, and a curtain.

There was lots of wildlife, around including bears, wolves, moose and deer. Ed and Molly's favourites were the deer. Each was given a name to fit its individual personality. In winter Ed would go off in the sleigh and cut cedar branches for the deer to eat. One special favourite they named Billy. For some reason, Billy took a dislike to Mary. One day she went to feed him some bread from her hand in the yard. For some reason, he knocked her over with his head and antlers. Several guests saw this happen and threw things at him to frighten him off. From then on Mary was terrified of Billy the deer, but no matter where she went, she was always running into him.

Sometimes in winter Mary would go with Ed to check his wolf trap lines. He had a permit to trap wolves, which were relatively common in the area. The only wolf he ever caught in two years was on a gorgeous moonlit night with the temperature way below zero. The wolf was a huge old one and seemed to have lost most of its teeth. Mary and Ed hadn't brought a sleigh with them so they had to trudge all the way back to the hotel to get one and drag the wolf carcass back. According to Mary,

> "It was like daylight and we could hear the wolves howling in the hills behind us. I kept telling Ed, 'Look, they're calling for their brother whom we've taken.'"[51]

---

[51]Interview with Mary Colson Clare, by Don Standfield, 1992, in the Ministry Archives.

It was a very eerie feeling for them. After the wolf was skinned and bounty recorded, Mary took the pelt and eventually made it into a coat, which she kept for many years. Even after Mary left Canoe Lake to work in Toronto she would come up to visit her uncle and aunt every Easter and Thanksgiving. She would either walk in from the Smoke Lake Hangar through the bush, with a pack on her back, or Ed would leave a canoe for her at the Canoe Lake landing and she'd paddle the four kilometers to Potter Creek without giving it a thought.

In 1933, the Ontario government began construction of Highway 60, which would run from Highway 11 just outside Huntsville to Barry's Bay. For this Depression-era government-sponsored project, workers toiled 10 hours a day, six days a week and earned the princely sum of $5 a month, plus board—a wage of roughly 2 cents an hour.[52] Completed in 1935, the dirt road was opened for business in 1936. In the early years the road was not much more than a trail full of crooked ruts. It had lots of low, swampy places, sharp curves and abrupt little hills and was maintained by a grader that would pass by three times a week. That first summer, 3,809 cars were checked in through the West Gate. From "Cache Lake to Whitney it was a bit rough but passable except after a heavy rain."[53]

In 1935, in anticipation of the highway's completion, Molly Colson realized that the days of the railway as the main access point were numbered and that there would likely be demand for services closer to the highway. She applied for a "license of occupation" to operate a canoe livery and store on a five-acre parcel of land at the south end of Canoe Lake at what was then called Portage Bay. It was given this name due to its easy access to the portage that led to Smoke Lake to the south. It took awhile to sort out the specific dimensions of the parcel and its use, so business that first year was likely conducted from a tent. Eventually the license was granted and a small log cabin on stilts was built in late 1937 or early 1938. The Portage Store came into being.[54]

The Portage Store had a long set of stairs that ran up the front to a little verandah. There was a small addition at the back containing a meat locker with ice. In the center of the room was a pot-bellied stove to keep the place warm during storms or cold weather. It was originally the supply depot for

---

[52]*Early Days in Algonquin Park*, pgs. 36-37.
[53]*The Raven*, June 1966, Vol. 7 # 2 (R.R). It wasn't until 1948 that Highway 60 was paved.
[54] There is conflicting evidence as to when the Portage Store was actually built. Shaw's book says it was built in 1936, yet Ministry correspondence suggests that in 1936 there was only a tent there.

Smoke and Canoe Lakes as most fishing trip outfitting still took place at the Colson Outfitting Store. The walls were lined with shelves full of basic supplies such as sugar, flour and tea. Molly would take orders for fresh food and the next week it would be delivered by Goldstein Truckers. The Colson's hired Joe Cousineau to manage the day-to-day operations, with daughters of various Canoe Lake leaseholders and residents helping out during the summer.

But managing both the Portage Store and Algonquin Hotel must have become too much for the Colsons, as in the spring of 1939 the Portage Store license, which included the store, a sleeping cabin and an icehouse, was transferred to Basil Hughes. Basil and his brother were apparently quite the characters. The two of them used to go off for days and leave a sign, "Gone Fishing," on the front door. One unsubstantiated story claimed that Hughes had a slot machine at the back of the store. A call came in from the Park Gate that the Ontario Provincial Police were coming in to raid the store and confiscate the machine. All of the men that were there that night grabbed the machine and carried it out into the bush. When the OPP arrived everyone pretended to have no idea that they were talking about. In 1941 Hughes went overseas to help with the war effort so the Colson family once again took over the management of the Portage Store and operated it until 1950 on a sublease basis.

Because there was now direct road access to Algonquin Park and to Canoe Lake along Highway 60, fewer and fewer people were taking the train. More and more visitors were launching their canoe trips to the interior from Portage Bay. The Portage Store got more involved in outfitting and in catering to visiting day tourists. Ed Colson would keep four or five chestnut canoes wrapped in burlap on a bed of straw out front to sell. Joe Cousineau and his daughter Lucille ran the day-to-day operations for a few summers. According to Mary Colson Clare, sometimes her mother Mary Colson (Ed's sister-in-law), would come and help. She loved Algonquin Park and for many summers was behind the counter, happy and cheery, smiling and joking. She knew everyone, so the Portage Store became the center of the social life at the south end. In the evenings, off-duty Wapomeo and Ahmek and Department staff would gather around eating ice cream, smooching penny candy and drinking soda that sat packed in ice in an old horse trough.

By 1943 the Colsons again decided that running both the Portage Store and the Algonquin Hotel was becoming too much to manage. They sold the hotel to George Merrydew, owner of a tavern in Toronto, and settled in an empty Omanique Lumber Company office near the northwest side of the trestle bridge at Potter Creek Bridge. Annie Colson left Algonquin Park and returned to her roots in Guelph where she later died. Today the only evidence that the Colson cabin existed is a lovely painting of it by leaseholder Irma Manning, which hangs on the wall of the Manning family cabin on Canoe Lake.

Molly Colson took ill in 1945 and died peacefully. As a tribute to her, the Canoe Lake and District Leaseholders Association placed a memorial brass plaque on the big island in Smoke Lake, which was her favourite picnicking and camping spot. From then on it became known as Molly's Island. More than 100 people came to pay their respects in July 1946 at the unveiling. Molly had been a major anchor of the local Algonquin Park community for nearly 50 years. The plaque contained the following inscription:

> **"Her spirit was one with the lakes and forests she loved – her heart and hands, ever at the service of those who called to her. Canoe Lake resident 1900 – 1945."**

In 1950 Ed Colson finally retired from the Portage Store and Basil Hughes sold the concession to Hilda Capp, a music teacher, and her accountant brother-in-law, Cardwell Walker. That fall, Capp requested permission from the Department to enlarge the facilities so that she could serve sandwiches and coffee, add a larger gift shop and possibly erect cabins to accommodate the growing number of overnight visitors. The Department wasn't very supportive of these ideas. In late 1951 she again wrote to the Department, this time to request permission to install a gas pump, fuel tanks and a pay phone. The pay phone was approved, but not the gas pump or tanks. There must have been demand for such a service as in 1953 she again wrote to ask for permission to sell gas from Imperial Oil and was again turned down.[55] This lack of interest by the Department in providing better services must have resulted in tremendous frustration and likely little profit. In 1954 she gave up and sold the lease to the group of Janey Roberts, Isobel Cowie, Marg McColl and Fran Smith, who became known as the "Ladies Who Ran the Portage Store."

---

[55]Correspondence in the Ministry Archives lease files.

Ed and Molly Colson, circa 1910—
APMA #5977 Florence Rich Adsit

Ed and Molly Colson, 1932—
APMA #5040 Mary Colson Clare

Panorama of Hotel Algonquin,
Colson Store and Joe Lake Station with Forest Fire Smoke Plume
likely circa 1930s—
APMA #4851 Mary Colson Clare

Hotel Algonquin

| ¶ Outfitting Store First-Class Canoe and Boat Livery. | IN ALGONQUIN PROVINCIAL PARK (OF ONTARIO) J. E. COLSON, PROPRIETOR | ¶ AT JOE LAKE STATION Ontario |

Joe Lake, Canoe Lake P. O., Ont. .... July 10th. 19 37

Hotel Algonquin—APMA #1398 Dr. D. M. Davison

Sign on Highway 60, circa late 1930s—
Gray Collection

Colson Outfitting Store—
APMA #1414 W.L. Bruce

Mary known as Molly Cox Colson in Pants, likely in 1920s—
APMA #2884—Mary Colson Clare

Ed & Molly Colson in Their Later Years—
APMA #6816 Mary Colson Clare

Annie Colson(right) & Mary Colson Clare—
APMA #3556 Mrs. W. Mooney

Lizzie Dennison (left) in
Hotel Algonquin Kitchen—APMA #5078 Mary Colson Clare

George Rowe's Cottage
Later Leased to Lila Stringer Grenke—
APMA #2947 Mrs. Calvert

George Rowe—
APMA #5084 Mary Colson Clare

Larry Dickson Outside His Cabin on Joe Creek—
APMA #2821 Doris Birch

Portage Store Looking North circa early 1930s—
APMA #4857 Mary Colson Clare

Portage Store Looking South circa late 1930s—
APMA #4858 Mary Colson Clare

The Ladies Who Ran the Portage Store (Marg McColl, Isobel Cowie, Janey Roberts & Fran Smith)

Portage Store
Viewed from the Parking Lot, 1953—
Noninski Collection

Marg McColl, Isobel Cowie, Janey Roberts and Fran Smith (Recollections by Isobel Cowie with contributions from Marg McColl, Janey Roberts and Islay McFarlane)

"How did four dumb women ever get hold of a gold mine like this?"

Marg McColl heard the American twang as she lay sunbathing on the dock of the Portage Store. She laughed to herself, for she was one of the four "dumb" women who owned the store in Algonquin Park. Marg, along with her friends Isobel Cowie and Janey Roberts had been introduced to Algonquin Park by a local Canoe Lake leaseholder, Frank Braucht, in the early 1940s.

Frank Braucht was born in Nebraska in 1878. He didn't talk much about his early life but newspaper articles from Guelph in the early 1950s indicated that at the age of 9 his family had moved from Nebraska to a ranch in Wyoming. As a boy he saw the last of the cowboy rounds ups and the Texas cattle trail herds. He even gained experience as a stage coach driver, carrying mail daily over a 35-mile route.[56] At the age of 19 he left Wyoming to get an education and in the early 1900s graduated from the University of Michigan with a Masters degree and a teaching certificate. He then went to the Philippines for several years before returning to teach both in Colorado and at the University of Michigan. He migrated north to Canada about 1913 to teach at Canada's first day technical school in Hamilton. After a decade in the Hamilton and Galt areas, Frank finally settled at Guelph Collegiate, where he taught vocational subjects until his retirement in 1949. He was a world traveler, visiting China, Japan and Mexico at a time when very few white faces ever ventured that far from home.

At an 1917 conference of the youth organization Older Boys, he heard Taylor Statten speak and became inspired to do boys' work. Eight years later, in 1925, he joined the Camp Ahmek staff and from then on he spent most of his summers at Taylor Statten Camps. For the first few summers he lived in a tent on a wooden platform on the hill just north of the old theatre site on Wigwam Bay. One year it was especially frosty in late August, so he built a stone fireplace and chimney at the end of his tent. Today that fireplace still stands and is incorporated into one of the Camp Ahmek staff cabins.

---

[56] Article in the Guelph Daily Mercury, June 25, 1949.

In 1932 he chose a lease site in the middle of Cook's Island. But after the lease was issued, the Park superintendent had a change of heart. Frank's front door view was going to be the Camp Wapomeo waterfront. The concern apparently was that his presence would "negatively impact the girls' privacy."[57] After what must have been significant back channel negotiations with the Department, Braucht was dissuaded from building on that site and in 1933 chose to build on what is now known as Lighthouse Point. Everett Farley built "Casa Mia" for him in 1934 out of peeled spruce logs, cut from the swamp behind the senior boys section at Camp Ahmek. As Frank wrote years later:

> "This humble cabin stands alone, by forest walls surrounded, but there is found a peace of soul, and happiness unbounded."[58]

Frank was a master craftsman at whatever he did. He built many of the Taylor Statten Camps' cabins. He also loved to carve wood and make furniture. His own cabin had a unique fireplace built by the McKinney Brothers from 900 pounds of stone shipped to him by the mines manager at Dome Mines as thanks for a stay at his cabin. McKinney was well known on the lake and also built the original fireplaces in the Ahmek dining hall and later at several other leaseholders in the area. Frank carved and mounted onto the front face, two iron thunderbirds filled with gold nuggets for eyes. The floors were covered with priceless rugs from Mexico, whose culture had strongly influenced him. He carved and crafted by hand all of the furniture, including a white pine table that was polished to a dark walnut finish. Around the edge of the table Frank carved a story using Navajo Indian symbols. He made two large chairs with Thunderbirds for backs. The birds were two-headed so that they could look out both sides.

In later years he added a boathouse, a small shower house, a cedar log ice house and a tent platform with two single beds equipped with mosquito netting for himself or overflow guests. In the early years he had a wooden box buried deep in the ground that when full of ice kept the fresh food cold and provided cold drinking water. He had running water long before hydro came in using a hand pump to maintain the proper pressure.

---

[57]Correspondence in the Ministry Lease Archives, 1933.
[58]Interviews with Islay McFarlane in 1999 and correspondence in the Ministry lease archives.

A fireplace nearby heated the water. But as one friend said,

> "It was murder when the pressure dropped during a shower.
> You had to pump the pressure back up by hand in order to
> get enough water to rinse off the soap."

Frank was a man apart. He did all of Wapomeo's repairs and often showed many on the lake how to fix things. He helped cottagers when their chimneys got overheated or when their water pipes burst. When new arrivals were building he'd stop by to observe the proceedings, willing to lend a hand or provide some advice or some missing tool. He lent his log cabin to people whom he considered the "right sort" for Algonquin Park. They included several women that went on to become long-time Canoe Lake residents. When visitors came Frank would retreat to his tent platform, have his meals at Wapomeo where he worked, and would occasionally look in to see how his guests were faring. All his guests were expected to help with various chores, including standing up to their waists in the water in the bay hauling out driftwood. According to his friends, he didn't want them to go soft. Among the most famous of his guests allegedly was Olive Diefenbaker, who came up every summer for 10 years and became the wife of John Diefenbaker, Canada's prime minister in the 1950s. She was known as Olive Palmer then and supposedly taught with Frank in Guelph. But Frank was a gruff sort. He didn't ever say much and when he did, he never wasted a word or spoke off colour. The strongest word anyone ever heard was one day when he was washing dishes in the kitchen at Wapomeo. A piece of flypaper broke loose from the ceiling and landed on his head and, according to Islay McFarlane, he let go an unprintable yell.

Frank was a great teacher and taught many on the lake skills for surviving in the bush. Some of the common refrains that Isobel Cowie remembered so well:

> "Never handle an axe that way! Want to spend the rest of
> your life with one leg? Always keep a chopping block be-
> tween you and the wood you're cutting!"

> "Don't dig your paddle as if you were hoeing potatoes! What
> the heck are you leaning so far forward for? It's as easy as
> walking; just keep your rhythm." That would have been at
> the end of a five-mile paddle!

"Come on now, you get the supper and Marg will paddle while I fish." And paddle Marg did, even though her arms were dropping off. And fish he did, so that for dinner they could have lake trout.[59]

Frank was also a scoutmaster and built a log adirondack shelter up the hill behind his place. He would bring up two or three carloads of scouts who would camp out for a week or two each summer, a practice that continued until 1961. The site was named Kamp Kayak after an old kayak given by Lou Handler, the owner of Camp Tamakwa on Tea Lake. One scout group had borrowed a few canoes from Camp Ahmek and paddled down to see the camp. While on a tour they came across the old tired out kayak. As they had no boats or canoes of their own, they were thrilled when Handler told them that they could have it so long as "he never had to see it again."

These scout groups were always very industrious. They blazed a trail to the Portage Store and constructed a diving tower for the dock during the Easter break in 1945. Another year they started to build his lighthouse. When it was completed in 1944, they added a hand-wound Victrola turntable to the top. It had been adjusted so that one full winding would turn the table for 26 hours. A rectangular box of red and clear glass (4" by 8" by 6") was installed on the top of the turntable, and a small coal oil lamp fastened inside. This enabled the lighthouse to emit light all night alternating bright white and red. In later years this was replaced by a battery powered intermittent flashing light.[60]

After he'd retired from teaching and the camps, he stayed at Canoe Lake from early spring until late fall. Frank was also a poet and used to hand-draw his Christmas cards each year on the blueprint paper used in draughting. He also wrote the commemorative poem on the Tom Thomson totem pole. In his later years he asked a long time friend and Canoe Lake visitor, Islay McFarlane, if she'd like his lease in return for keeping an eye out for him. Islay McFarlane had first come to Canoe Lake as a bookkeeper at Taylor Statten Camps. Her ex-husband, Jack McFarlane, had been a teacher at Lawrence Park Collegiate in Toronto and had been hired to run the waterfront program. She spent six years in the late 1950s and '60s at Camp Wapomeo. Islay was another Canoe Lake independent spirit. She

---

[59]The Portage Store, unpublished manuscript by Isobel Cowie, found in 2000.
[60]The lighthouse is carefully maintained today by a neighbour and friend, Chuck Gray.

was best friends with Elsie Ridpath, Fran Roe and Ruth Clark. The "girls" would fish together for hours on end near Popcorn Island. For many summers Islay cooked Frank his meals, managed all the housekeeping tasks and kept an eye on him.

After Frank's death in 1968, at age 90, Islay stayed on by herself every summer. Unfortunately in the winter of 1976, "Casa Mia" was struck by lightning and burned to the ground. Passersby were able to save much of the furniture. Later, the one remaining sleeping cabin that Frank used in his later years was transferred to the Matthews' site and Islay continued to come to Canoe Lake every summer until her death in 2000. Though the lighthouse still stands under the diligent care of a local resident, all that remains at the site today is the ruined shell of a small icehouse and the fireplace. The point is used occasionally for a picnic or a swim by visitors who have no idea as to its rich history.

Frank had invited Marg, Isobel and Janey, as was his frequent custom for those whom he deemed "suitable," up for a week's holiday. Marg was an elementary school teacher and Isobel was a high school teacher, active in Girl Guides and CGIT. As Isobel stated in her memoirs of Canoe Lake:

> "Our love affair with Algonquin began the year of the Battle of Britain at Frank Braucht's cabin. There were six of us that time in Frank's 'harem.' While the battle roared, one of the girls, Ella Sinclair reported it blow by blow from the radio hooked up to the clothesline. Marg and I were heartbroken, for many of our students were engaged in the fighting. Each week brought news of more casualties. We were on holidays and didn't want to waste a precious moment, so tried to find peace from conflict in the beauty of the Park. We went canoeing at every opportunity in Frank's lovely craft, with its Indian motif on the border.

> "Frank had hauled a piano in over the snow one winter, so Wam Stringer a local fiddler and pianist would arrive each evening to play for the assembled crowd. It was a wild time and we made the best of it. One evening two cooks from Camp Ahmek came to escort us to a local dance. They came to pick us up dressed in pristine white slacks and shirts. They

looked quite handsome with their slicked back hair and eyes shining. Unfortunately, when we were about to depart, one stepped off of the dock into the canoe and he lost his footing. He went splashing into the water. Alas, he couldn't swim, so Marg was obliged to jump in after him and save him. This didn't daunt him as he retired to Frank's cabin and reappeared in borrowed grey and off we went once more. Later we found out that they were Germans and had been arrested soon after and taken away for questioning. We often wondered what happened to them, but had no way of finding out."[61]

After many years of vacationing at Frank's "Casa Mia," Marg and Isobel leased one of the last sites available on Canoe Lake in 1953. The site was rocky, covered with brush and very little was flat. The Huntsville surveyor who came to officially survey the site wrote to them later to complain. It had apparently taken him two days to recuperate from his day spent climbing up and down the cliff to perform the needed measurements. The next summer, Marg's brother Bob had a holiday and agreed to spend it helping them build a cabin. His 8-year-old son Paul came along as handyman. To arrange for the building supplies, Marg tentatively ventured into the Huntsville Planing Mill, which at the time was a bastion of maleness. She cornered a genial chap in the lumberyard and asked him what could be built for the $300 that she had. He hemmed and hawed and quickly sketched a rudimentary building with walls, windows, roof and doorway. He then calculated the amount of needed lumber, shingles and nails and they were in business. Marg handed over her $300 and a few days later the materials arrived at the leaseholders' dock. Unfortunately the weather at Canoe Lake was not cooperative. Just as the group arrived and pitched a tent on the lease site, a terrible thunderstorm broke. As Marg recounted later,

> "Never had we seen such lightning, flashing brilliantly across the black clouds nor heard the thunder roar with such strength. It was as if the heavens didn't want this project. For the next week it rained as only in Algonquin it can rain. Everything was soaking wet and the bloodthirsty mosquitoes came out in droves. It took all of Bob's

---

[61]The Portage Store, an unpublished manuscript by Isobel Cowie.

workmanship to secure dry wood for the campfire, though we did have a Coleman stove, which made cooking a touch easier. Bob began the clearing of the land even in the rain, and the rest of us helped as we could. Our hands were soon sore from dragging the brush. Horrid, stubborn stuff, it got stuck in roots and stones, scratched our faces and tore at our clothing. In the chill of the morning young Paul would huddle by the spruce trees, shivering miserably, hugging himself for warmth. The lumber we had ordered from Huntsville appeared at the Portage Store dock. We lashed Frank's canoe to ours and made a raft. The lumber was piled on top and to the amazement of other cottagers, we paddled the whole thing across the lake to our cabin site. We then hauled all of that wood up the cliff. Only once, when paddling over the foundation timbers, did we almost get defeated. The wind caught the wood and blew us out into the main part of the lake. We were powerless to get back to shore. Luckily a neighbour saw our distress and came out in his boat to tow us back to shore."[62]

After two weeks of furious work the basics of the cabin were completed. Marg and Isobel sat in the doorway with their feet hanging over the edge, savouring their hard work and rejoicing at their triumph. Their tiny cabin built of cedar they had hauled across a lake and through the bush, stood on ground cleared with their own hands. There was no power to drive electrical equipment, so every board had been sawn and hammered by hand. It was a glorious feeling. Later McColl and Cowie reportedly heard through the Canoe Lake grapevine that other women on the lake complained about their efforts. They were concerned that soon their men folk would be insisting on their working in this way as well.

The huge pile of brush that they cleared took three summers to burn. They attacked it whenever they had a little bit of free time. What a pleasant feeling it was when it was finally done. Occasionally, over the years, trees would become a problem. One year a huge hemlock up on the cliff started to lean out over the cabin, threatening its safety. Bob decided it was too dangerous to leave. He shinnied up the long trunk, threw a rope, near the

---

[62] Memories of Isobel Cowie's Algonquin Days pg 6.

top and told Marg, Fran, Paul and Isobel to hold on to the end of it as he sawed the bottom. When he shouted "Go!" they were to drop the rope end and run. At one point in the task, Paul, Marg's young nephew, inquired as to what would happen if he hung on. He was advised in no uncertain terms that he'd likely go catapulting out into the lake. Bob did a great job. The tree fell cleanly along the north side of the cabin. Later it provided a good feeding spot for the birds. Frequently, in the morning, the girls would hear the *tap-tap-tap* of huge pilleated woodpeckers lined up on the trunk, enjoying their breakfast.

Later Bob built bunk beds, cupboards and a beautiful pine table with chairs to match for inside the main cabin. A few years later they added a bunkee and a boathouse. The boathouse was built out over the water but contained camp beds instead of boats. According to Isobel it was a joy to sleep down there with windows wide open to the north. They would watch the "northern lights" at night and listen at dawn to the chorus of chickadees and white-throated sparrows calling *"chickadee-dee-dee"* and *"canada-canada."* In the evenings, if they were quiet, the loons would swim past the dock, their young perched on their backs, looking for an evening meal. A long line of a dozen or so merganser ducks would silently paddle past as would the occasional beaver. As they walked up to the main cabin each morning, woodpeckers would hammer at the fallen logs, hummingbirds would come darting out as soon as the feeder was put out and a ruffed grouse would drum its song on the top of a rock near the cabin. Whiskey Jacks came to visit looking for food and blue jays, their saucy cousins, would dart down onto their picnic table to taste the butter and steal the bread crumbs. A scarlet tanager would flaunt its beauty on occasion, and rose-breasted grosbeaks would adorn the maple trees after a rain.

There was lots of other wildlife too. Otters played by the boathouse, giant bull frogs would honk in the bay, and even the occasional snapping turtle would invade their waters. The chipmunks would creep out and help themselves to the remains of the breakfast porridge on the path near the back door. That porridge was a special mixture of rolled oats and Red River cereal that they found out later canoe trippers loved. One summer, Isobel's nephew told his parents that he had dreamed of "Aunt Isobel's porridge." His father offered to make it for him and was promptly advised that there was "no way that he'd be able to make it like Aunt Isobel did."[63]

---

[63]Ibid, pg. 8.

Both Marg and Isobel were avid fisherwomen and as luck would have it their cabin turned out to be next to one of the finest fishing holes on Canoe Lake. This was because it was located on the edge of a bay that was virtually filled with deadheads left over from the changes in the waterline 50 years before. The fish loved to hide in and around the dead stumps. At 11 a.m. on a typical morning, Isobel would go down to the dock, throw in her fishing line and have enough bass caught and cleaned by lunchtime. They later discovered that the lake trout lurked on a certain line from the store to Gilmour Island. As Isobel said, "One of the finest presents one could receive was one of those beauties."

One day Paul and Marg were out trolling and caught a beauty. It almost knocked Marg out of the canoe with its tail, but they handily reeled it in. Like many others, the two of them were disgruntled when a strange boat came on the lake for only an hour or two and the occupants were lucky enough to catch a big one. They felt this was cheating the residents. One of their friends was an ardent fisherman. One day he was fishing on one of the smaller lakes nearby, when he saw a cloud of fish raining from the sky. Worrying terribly that he was hallucinating, he was later relieved when he discovered that it was just the Department seeding the lake.

Bears were also unfortunately frequent visitors. One spring a bear tore off the back door to the cabin not once, but twice. Everything inside was shattered except for one set of Marg's favourite dishes with their pattern of a Jack-in-the-pulpit. The arborite counter top was ripped up, the lower cupboard doors were all broken, their handles bent. Though repaired later, the teeth marks remained on the cupboard and on a chest that held Marg's silver. There were vivid signs of his marauding. To make matters worse, Marg went up to inspect the roof and to everyone's horror, a step on the ladder gave way and she fell to the porch floor and broke her leg. Janey and Isobel rushed her to the Huntsville Hospital where her leg was placed in an uncomfortable and unwieldy cast. Marg was forced to spend the rest of the summer, laid up on the porch or the dock.

Marg and Isobel were more afraid of moose than of bears. All of the bears that they had ever met would leave after some harassment. But moose were temperamental. One never knew what they would do. One morning Isobel was at the woodpile and heard Marg say softly from the door, "Stay where you are." Down the path from the north came a female moose and her baby. What beautiful creatures they were! Their coats shone in the sun like velvet. As moose don't see very well, it wasn't apparent that they were aware of either of the women, frozen in place nearby. Another time a huge bull-moose with a full rack of antlers stood majestically on the hill one morning as they came out of the lake from their swim. He dared them to approach, but they ducked into the boathouse. Later they saw him swimming across the lake, his antlers rearing proudly above the water. On Highway 60 moose were then, and still are today, a menace. The animals would graze in swamps along the highway. So many motorists would stop to see them, that there would be traffic jams and imminent danger of collisions. One year they heard that the Park rangers wouldn't drive the access road from one of the lakes after dark, because there had been so many accidents involving vehicles and moose.

In the fall of 1954, Marg and Isobel heard that the Portage Store was for sale and along with their friends Fran Smith and Janey Roberts, convinced a bank manager to loan them the money to buy it with their houses in Guelph as collateral. For three summers, from 1955 to 1957, the "Ladies Who Ran the Portage Store" rented out canoes and sold groceries, ice and massive amounts of ice cream to local cottagers, canoe trippers and tourists. It was a tremendous learning experience for them all. Isobel recounted this wonderful story about their early days:[64]

> "Can I see one of your worms?"
>
> Startled, we looked over the counter to see a small five-year-old gazing up at us expectantly. Janey gulped, but obligingly went down to the cellar and brought plump, lively worms for his inspection.
>
> "I'll take that one."
>
> The youngster pointed to a fat dew worm and put a nickel on the counter. Satisfied, he strode off with long steps for his fishing expedition.
>
> "You could have given him one," I remonstrated.
>
> "No," said Fran. "We're in business. We sell, not give. How many more youngsters would we have asking for worms, otherwise?"

---

[64] Ibid, pg. 2.

And sell we did. Everything from mukluks to groceries. Ice cream cones by the score . . . 1,000 one day. Our arms ached from dipping them!

Though banks at the time were willing to loan money to buy a business with a house as collateral, they were less willing to provide the operating capital. As Isobel recounted,

"When we asked the bank manager for further money to buy our first load of groceries, he remarked, 'Well I knew I was taking a risk with the principal, but I really didn't expect to pay for the stock, also.'"

The groceries though were the lifeblood of the community. "The Ladies" sold bread and milk in high volume for only 1 cent over cost but these commodities presented a number of challenges.[65] The milk, which came from Huntsville, was particularly hard to deal with. It was often sour by the time it reached them, as there were no refrigerated trucks in those days. Bread too was difficult. Sometimes they didn't have enough, at others, they were overstocked. Once when they had a surplus, they put the stale bread out behind the store for the deer. That night they had a "stag party" that they never forgot. Twenty or more bucks gathered for dinner, the moonlight glistening on their antlers.

Horace, a green grocer from Toronto, would appear once a week with a truck loaded down with fresh fruits and vegetables. The women on the lake usually would corner him first and would leave little for the store. Fresh meat was at a premium, but "The Ladies" had an obliging butcher in Huntsville who would take their meat orders and bring them a truck load every once in awhile. Packages of "minute steaks" would be piled high in the fridge as steak orders were popular in summer. Isobel hated butcher delivery days as it was her job to stack the meat. When finished, her hands would be dripping in blood. Fran boasted that they always delivered orders to their customers on time. As she said,

"Only once did we slip up. A woman from Smoke Lake had ordered pork tenderloin for special guests, but she didn't come and didn't come for her order. A week went by, and then another, so I brought the package to the

---

[65]Ibid, pg 17.

kitchen and suggested to our delighted cook Anne, that we have them for dinner as they would have spoiled otherwise. Of course, as expected, the next morning the woman appeared demanding her order. When she found out that we had eaten it, she made a cutting remark about our wonderful efficiency and stamped out in disgust. She returned the next week of course, as we were her only source of supply."[66]

Bordens Dairy[67] supplied them their ice cream. Naturally, many visitors had the same question about Bordens ice cream:

> "Do you have Lady Borden in a tub?"
> "Yes, certainly," would be our reply.
> To which they would respond, "Then, let her out!"

The Bordens salesman showed them exactly how to dip a cone – one scoop, carefully rounded. Marg's nephew Paul was the only one to perfect the technique. The others would make cones that were considered far too lavish. The Bordens freezer was supposed to only be used for ice cream, but space was limited so they were often forced to break their regulations. Whenever the Bordens truck appeared the helpers would run to give warning. The meat would be quickly taken out of the ice cream case and passed from hand to hand and piled haphazardly in the food freezer. Of course, the drivers likely knew what was happening, but they never let on. According to Isobel, once the ice cream freezer wasn't working properly, and the repairman arrived to put in a new motor. Marg and Janey asked him in for lunch as it was just past noon. When he went out to finish the job, the motor had disappeared. Later in the week, one of the cottagers was in the store boasting about the marvelous new motor that her handyman had just put in her refrigerator. They knew instantly what had happened.

As "The Ladies" learned how to manage a business through trial and error, their local customers were wonderful and helpful in many ways. One leaseholder from the north end of the lake would help frequently with ice cut from the lake in the winter. It was packed in sawdust and stored in the ice house. He would take on the difficult task of getting the ice blocks out,

---

[66] Ibid, pg. 5.
[67] Ibid, pg. 14.

and then sawing them into the halves or quarters that customers wanted. Elsie Ridpath, another local, helped diversify the Portage Store offerings by bringing some treasures from her Toronto furniture store for them to sell. The lamps and other antiques were real drawing cards and eagerly sought. Another woman made beautiful silver bracelets that flew off of the shelves. That first summer, many of the local cottagers made large deposits on their accounts so that "The Ladies" would have enough cash flow. It was most thoughtful, but very confusing for the helpers. A "McCaskey system," a set of cards with each person's name on it, normally used to keep track of how much credit was being provided to each customer, was used by "The Ladies" in reverse. They would deduct sales from the total amount deposited by the customer.

Fran and Isobel checked the books and counted every last coin each night so even with this system, they didn't get into too much trouble. Isobel said, though, that their attitude to money changed over time.

> "Eventually we got weary of counting every coin and would just count the bills but even that became tiresome. One night when the four of us owners sought peace at our cabin on the lake, Marg and I suddenly remembered the bag with our day's money in it.
>
> "Did you bring it up from the dock?" Marg queried.
>
> "No, I didn't – did you?", I answered back.
>
> "No!", was Isobel's reply
>
> So there it sat until the next morning – we were too tired to redeem it. A strong wind would have blown it into the water.[68]

---

[68]Ibid, pg. 15.

Each Monday, Isobel was delegated to take the money to the bank in Huntsville, with stern instructions not to pick up any hitchhikers. But one cold morning she came upon a pitiful sight. A man with his wife and two children were shivering by their car, which had broken down. She forgot the rules and bundled them into her car. They had been stranded there all night, so she took them to the nearest garage. Afterwards she repented, for the smell from their unwashed bodies was so strong it took days to get rid of it. One year Fran had to return to Guelph for weekdays as her mother was ill. The remaining trio promised to call her if they ever reached $1,000 in one day's sales. Sure enough, one day they did and they phoned her triumphantly. There was a celebration that night, and the help received a well-deserved bonus. What a difference from the beginning![69]

Another amusing story that Isobel loved to tell involved the pop machine. By the end of it where the lids of the pop cans were taken off, stood a fire bucket, usually with dirty water in it. They had a money drawer just over it, and one day, one of the helpers, pulled the drawer out too far and all of the money fell into the bucket.

"John, you'll just have to take that money out and wash it," Marg demanded.

So John, who later became a high school principal, and member of Parliament, repaired to the back of the store chuckling.

"Never thought I'd have to launder dirty money!"[70]

Marg was the super salesperson of the group. She always had special customers who would wait patiently until she was free. One was a bit indiscreet and once shouted loudly, "I want that woman with the green bottom to wait on me!" Marg never wore those shorts every again. One American cottage owner was not exactly pleased when Isobel had to do the honours of waiting on her one day. The woman wanted toilet paper but was too embarrased to say so, so asked instead for 'rose petals.' Poor Isobel had no idea what rose petals were. All she could think of were rose buds, those small chocolate candies. The after hours discussion of the resulting clarification dialogue had everyone in stitches with laughter for weeks.

---

[69]Ibid, pg. 16.
[70]Ibid, pg. 15.

One item that they couldn't keep in adequate supply was mukluks. These were oiled moccasins that were wonderful on the trails. Marg's nephew Paul and another summer helper Bill were their chief salesmen. If they were too small a fit, Paul assured the customer that they would stretch in the rain. If they were too big, Bill averred that they would shrink in the rain. Marg told a marvelous story of a shoe shopping expedition on Fifth Avenue in New York. She went into a high-class store and the clerk was most helpful.

"You need them for work?" he inquired.

"Yes, please," Marg responded.

"What have you been wearing lately?" he enjoined.

"Mukluks," Marg replied, without breaking a smile.

"Mukluks?" he inquired with a quizzical look on his face.

"Yes, you know, oiled moccasins," Marg said.

"Oh, do you walk to work?" he asked.

"Oh, no! We canoe in each morning and I'd really like something more glamorous," she replied.

The clerk looked at her carefully. A squaw from Ontario? And red-headed? Marg departed with slim, high-heeled dancing shoes, as the clerk shook his head in amazement.

"Wait until I tell the boys about this!" he chortled to himself. [71]

Sometimes Marg would sell things that she wasn't supposed to sell. One day Bill was anxiously searching for his favourite hat. Trying to be helpful, Marg started querying him as to where he might have left it. When he told her that he'd left it hanging on a peg in the kitchen a frown came over her face. In a small voice she told him that she hadn't thought it had belonged to anyone and had sold it to a canoe tripper going up the lake the previous day. She promised to get him another in Huntsville. Bill wasn't easily

---

[71] Ibid, pg. 6.

mollified but was too polite to give his real feelings expression. Another time she sold a copy of the Atlantic Monthly that Isobel had driven 70 miles to get.

"Well, he needed something decent to read!" she exclaimed at the time.

Even her own new shorts went to a woman who was roasting in heavy slacks. Another funny incident was the time a new Canadian entered the store and asked for "Aggs." Isobel thought he meant an axe and proceeded to bring a hatchet down from the stairway. He then tried to explain again. It wasn't until Marg overheard the discussion that it finally got sorted out that he was looking for eggs – not an axe.

But the ultimate story was the incident with the white fox fur. Early one morning as Marg was scrubbing the store floor, the bell over the door tinkled and a quartet came in, the two women shivering from the cold rain, the men placating.

"Miss, could I see that white fox fur you have hanging up over there?"

Marg rose from her knees and brought it down for their inspection.

"Would you model it, Miss?"

So Marg, shorts and blouse dripping with water, her hair hanging over her red face, casually flung the fur over her shoulders and paraded around the room. "Like it, honey?" the rugged, burly type inquired of the dizzy blonde.

"No!" she snapped.

"Aw honey, just try it on," he pleaded.

"NO!" And she turned and left the store.

The man apologised profusely, and with his friends, followed the irate woman out the door. Marg went back to her scrubbing. A few minutes later, the door opened again, and the quartet reappeared.

"Would you try that on again, Miss?"

Swallowing her temper, Marg donned the fur and once again modeled it, fuming at the blonde's scathing glance.

"Well?" prompted Mr. Charming. "Oh, all right!", exclaimed the blonde.

"How much, Miss?", the chastened man asked

"Five dollars", was Marg's gruff reply.

Smiling broadly, the gallant produced the money, satisfied that he might now be able to resume his thwarted canoe trip. That was a bargain, for the white fur was one of a consignment flown directly from the Arctic by Marg's flyer boyfriend.[72]

Janey was responsible for looking after the canoes rented to canoe trippers going to the interior or visitors out for day paddles around the lake. It was quite a difficult job because many people booked them one or two weeks in advance. The boys checked the canoes as they came in, and repaired any minor damage. Once a chap came in, holding six paddles in a bunch in his hand. Something warned Janey, so she inspected them before putting them back on the racks. One paddle was taped together after having been broken in half, and another was badly split. She had to work hard to convince the renter that he should pay for the damage. She had the renter's car license plate number so had the upper hand and the matter was eventually resolved. One weekend they were all out of canoes. Late at night, a Toronto doctor came in desperate to have one. Trying to be helpful, Marg suggested he take her old canoe but warned him that it was long and heavy. He told her that he'd take anything, as he just had to get away for the weekend. The following Tuesday morning, he returned from his camping trip exhausted and quite bent out of shape. He told Marg in no uncertain terms that she shouldn't ever rent that canoe out to anyone ever again. He'd apparently had to drag it over the portages, it was such a dead weight. At one point he even suggested that Marg ought to pay him for taking it!

Ordering supplies was Isobel's responsibility. The staff claimed that she worked it so that she could have time off fraternizing in the back storage room with the salesmen. The salesmen were an obliging group, always

---

[72]Ibid, pg. 3.

helpful with suggestions. Magazines and books were supplied by a Huntsville firm and were a problem. The company insisted on also sending sizzling hot cheap-sex romances, not suited for a store with dignity, Isobel thought. But Marg, as usual, saved some for a cottager who longed for them. This same firm also sent the daily Globe and Mail newspaper. One canoe tripper saved his money by reading the paper in the store. He really didn't need to, for one day, after his canoe overturned, he came into the store to put his bills out on the counter to dry. The staff's eyes bulged as he spread out his American $20 and $50 bills along its length. Why he didn't want to spend a few cents on the newspaper was very curious.

National Grocers, a delivery company, brought in supplies weekly. When their truck appeared, everyone rushed to help. Boxes upon boxes were carried up the steps to the storage room. On hot July days it was a steaming task. The canoe trippers were particularly fond of cookies, but twice Isobel accidentally double-ordered. They had cookies everywhere – in the storage space, in the office, even in the sleeping quarters. No one complained and eventually they all were sold. On one occasion they had sold so much stock that the shelves were empty. They had to lock the door to keep customers out while they re-stocked. The customers had no patience whatever. The nasty remarks that were said would make a saint's ears and cheeks turn red. The same would happen when "The Ladies" took the occasional Sunday morning off and had a cook-out somewhere on the lake. By the time they returned in the afternoon, customers would be lined up like vultures.

The pot-bellied stove was a major draw, especially in inclement weather. When the store first opened in the chilly days of the early summer, cottagers would stand around and tell jokes, tall stories and in general recount their adventures. Their laughter and jovial dispositions set a happy tone for the season and helped everyone over many a weary day. One leaseholder claimed that he was successfully hunting for precious gems in the Park, but no one ever saw any of his prizes. He would boast that it was Pabulum that kept him fit and able to do his extensive prospecting. One morning this same fellow followed Marg into their sleeping quarters at the back of the store, and asked for a blanket. The eyebrows of everyone in the store went up, wondering what the old coot was up to. When questioned, he quickly explained that his wife had fallen into the water when they went to get into the boat to come down to the store and was now getting cold. Cold! That morning it was freezing. The wretch had left her shivering outside while he doddered about his business in the store. Perhaps it was revenge, for later he was always having to use the store pay phone to call long distance to Toronto to get her to send him money whenever he left her in the city.[73]

Other frequent visitors were the campers from the children's camps all around. They were always a happy lot and so were "The Ladies" when they counted their sales after they'd gone. The little campers would arrive in their large war canoes and quickly fill the store demanding their treats. Their helper Bill warned that one of the campers' favourite sports was to try and get their booty free. They'd get a bag at one end of the store, fill it with their treasures, carry it to the other end, and make off with their prize in the crowd. But the Portage Store staff bested them by keeping the bag and filling it for the children as they made their purchases. "Twizzlers" were one of their favourites. One year the camp doctor was worried and came down to inspect them. He diagnosed them safe, concluding that they were just licorice and glue. One day, one camper decided that he wanted 100 and was thoroughly frustrated when Carol, age 7, who was "helping out," mounted on a stool behind the counter took forever to count them out. Halfway through the boy got antsy and in a huff told her to forget it. She bristled that if he did so she'd wrap them around his neck. He waited patiently until she was finished.

The living quarters of "The Ladies" left much to be desired. The boys slept in a huge tent behind the store. They often retired there for a short nap if the day was not too busy. The helpers and Anne the cook (Marg's sister) slept above the main store and the four owners slept in a lean-to at the back of the store. Mice were a particular problem. They rattled the lids on all of the pots in the kitchen and they could never catch them all. Those they did catch they threw out, traps and all, rather than handle them. Fran was always afraid to go to sleep, worried that a mouse might enter her mouth if she snored. One night it rained hard, and Marg awakened to find a foot of water around her pillow. That was the night Isobel almost left the business, for a wet mouse ran across her face, dragging its wet tail. Another time one of the customers looked up one day as a shower of water fell on the counter in front of her. It turned out not to be a leak in the roof, at all. It was just one of the helpers who had flung her wet bathing suit on the floor.

They had room to accommodate quite a few people, but the record was achieved in the summer of 1957, when nineteen people, cut off from other

---

[73]Ibid, pg. 9.

places stayed the night. It was the Canada Day weekend and Hurricane Audrey had hit Ontario.

> "So much water fell that it overwhelmed many of the area beaver dams. The ones holding back March Hare Lake east of the Camp Ahmek waterfront at the north end of the lake broke. A huge wall of water went pouring down the rocky gorge which led to Hickey Creek (now called Wigwam Bay). That flood of water plus overflow at Joe Lake Dam made the water level in Canoe Lake rise over 3 feet."[74]

At the south end, the Thompsons' fireplace was completely underwater and they were even able to paddle the canoe under the front porch to inspect the footings under the house. At one cabin, the storm brought down 17 trees and a neighbour had to paddle out and erect a flag to mark the end of the dock. At another, the wife got up to feed her baby in the middle of the night and had to run out in the wind and rain to pull the canoe halfway up the hill so that it would be above the high-water mark. The flood swamped Potter Creek and put a foot of mud on many of the cabin floors. One resident, Pappy Stringer, refused to leave the house, so his son Wam paddled in the front door to rescue him from the kitchen. The story goes that on his way out the door, Wam stopped at the piano and played a few tunes. At the Portage Store, the flood nearly ruined "The Ladies'" business. The building was creaking at its foundations and they were terribly worried that it would collapse. Everything in the cellar was afloat including the worms, cabbages, lettuce and carrots. Nevertheless, "The Ladies" put on a brave front and rowed out to the end of the submerged dock to hoist the Canadian flag on July 1. The American visitors cheered their patriotism.[75]

In 1956 the group requested permission to build an outhouse and install gas pumps. The outhouse was approved, but the gas pumps were not. In those days, "The Ladies" used to pump the gas by hand from 10 50-gallon drums into smaller containers, which were then poured into the car gas tanks. It was terribly hard and very time consuming. In 1957 they asked to

---

[74]Lundell, L. (editor), Lloyd, D. (concept), *Fires of Friendship: Eighty Years of the Taylor Statten Camps*, Fires of Friendship Books, Toronto, pg. 130.
[75]The Portage Store, memories of Isobel Cowie, pg. 11.

extend the kitchen to provide a screened-in porch to serve meals for the staff and to install gas pumps. This time they emphasized that it would be a safer way to dispense gas and would lessen their work considerably. Finally the Department agreed that it would be beneficial to the public during the summer season to be able to stop and get gas at one location along Highway 60. A contract was signed with Imperial Oil, which installed a gas pump in May 1957. However, by this time, after three summers of backbreaking work, the friends were tired out. It was also becoming apparent that the 1954 government policy of not renewing leases meant that the Department now wanted more control over commercial activities in the Park.

Unbeknownst to them, the Department had in fact decided that the Portage Store property needed to be acquired and replaced with a more modern building to be managed on a concession basis. "The 'Ladies" were under great pressure from the Department to sell out, but they were unwilling to do so for the "paltry sum" that the Department was offering.[76] The negotiations must not have gone well as there is a note in the lease archives suggesting that the Department was going to:

> "Take the matter to the Advisory Committee of the Ontario
> Parks Integration Board." The plan was to "get permission
> to build a modern outfitting and eating establishment close
> to the present store to be run on a concession basis."[77]

This implied threat to the "The Ladies'" franchise must have been enough. The property was acquired by the Department shortly afterward for significantly less than what was asked. The old store was torn down. A new structure was built, and open for business in 1960, with Ken Simpson running an expanded concession that included a grocery store, canoe trip outfitting depot, gift shop, motorboat and canoe rentals and gasoline sales.[78]

After their Portage Store ownership experiences, Marg and Isobel retired to their cabin on the lake. The friends never did get the hydro connected. Marg wrote decades later in an unpublished article that they learned the art of doing without.

---

[76]Correspondence found in the Ministry lease archives.
[77]Ibid.
[78]Ken Simpson of Toronto ran the concession until 1974 when it was leased by Alquon Ventures Inc. (Eric and Sven Miglin) and managed by Eric Sultmanis.

The Art of Doing Without[79]

Who in this last decade of the 20th Century in central Ontario lives without electricity? We do! We always intended to have it put in, but for two months of the year, why bother? Especially when it costs a fortune to have enough poles put in to carry the lines from our neighbours. So we managed with gas lamps until we had propane put in. Just for a two-burner stove, and two lights for the cabin. One has to shift the table for euchre so that no one is in complete darkness. When the propane tank emptied one night, we used a coal oil lamp – very dim! Plumbing? Oh no! We have a line from the lake to a pump outside the cabin and of course an outdoor privy. A little inconvenient in the rain, but sufficient. For bathing, there is always the lake. We told a woman at the Huntsville Laundromat that we swam first thing in the morning. She stared at us and said, "What are you, English or something!" We have no refrigeration, just a cooler. We buy the ice at the Portage Store for $1.75 a bag, and then go 70 miles for groceries every 10 days or so. In compensation, we have plenty of fresh air, warm sun and friends who are always at hand to help. On any day, we have more social calls than we ever have in the city. The hummingbirds often come to the feeder, the squirrels for the peanuts on the porch and the chipmunks for the leftover porridge on a stone. It's our own spot of sanity in a mad world."

Fran returned to Guelph and took up a new career as a business professional. She and Janey belonged to the local Business and Professional Women's Club and were Bridge and badminton partners for many years. A couple of years later Janey Roberts acquired a lease up the east shore. Marg and Isobel remained on Canoe Lake until Marg's death. Soon after Isobel sold the cabin and has not returned. As she said:

"Those days were precious intervals. The sound of the loon echoing over the lake will be forever imprinted on my mind. Algonquin's melody – mystical and eerie."

---

[79] Notes by Marg McColl found in 2000.

Isobel Cowie (left) and
Marg McColl (right)—
Gray Collection

Marg McColl (left) and
Isobel Cowie (right)—
Gray Collection

Birthday Party, Marg McColl (left),
Isobel (right)—Gray Collection

Janey Roberts in Later Years—
Gray Collection

Frank Braucht's Casa Mia, circa 1930s—
Matthews/McFarlane Collection

Navajo Indian Legends in Casa Mia, 1933—Frank Braucht

Frank Braucht next to his Thunderbird Fireplace, circa 1940s—
Matthews/McFarlane Collection

Frank Braucht Demonstrating the
Indian Stroke, circa 1940s—
Matthews/McFarlane Collection

Frank Braucht Dressed in
Native Costume, circa 1940s—
Matthews/McFarlane Collection

Frank Braucht Showing How to
Carry a Canoe Solo—
Gray Collection

Frank Braucht Holding Freshly
Caught Fish—Gray Collection

Frank Braucht's Lighthouse,
2000—Clemson Collection

Portage Store, 1963—APMA #925 MNR

Portage Store Dock Area after Hurricane Audrey in 1957—Gray Collection

Edith Webb

Rimmer/Webb Boathouse in Winter 1950s—
Gray Collection

Edith Webb

Another woman resident for a time on Canoe Lake maintained a little business renting out cabins and canoes to visitors. She would charge $1.50 per day per canoe to day-trippers who used the south end of Canoe Lake as a launching pad for a day of paddling and picnicking. It was a much less intimidating lake than Smoke Lake and a marvelous day could be had by paddling the circuit south from Canoe Lake, through Bonita Narrows, Bonita Lake to Tea Lake and then east through the Smoke Creek channel to the Smoke Lake Landing. If they were unwilling to retrace the route a short portage from the Smoke Lake Leaseholders Landing would return them to the south end of Portage Bay.

Edith Webb, known as Miss Webb, had inherited in 1939 a lease on the first northwest point out of Portage Bay from a family friend, Robert Rimmer. Her father apparently built several of the fireplaces on the site, so must have been well-known to Rimmer. Rimmer had taken out the lease in 1920 after he retired from the Department of Lands and Forests, at which he had worked since 1909. Borrowing $1,000 from his neighbour across the lake, John Macklem, he built a lovely log cabin with a screened-in porch. He was a well-known, highly regarded bachelor with a likeable personality and many acquaintances and deemed to be "very smooth in conversation."[80] He had come to Canada as a "Home Boy" about the time of the Crows Nest Pass construction and had found life difficult in Canada. He lived at Canoe Lake for most of the year with occasional visits to friends in Hamilton. According to George Garland, a long-time Smoke Lake resident, Rimmer also worked as a timekeeper during the construction of Highway 60 when there were camps at both Tea Lake Dam and on the site that eventually became the Smoke Lake Hangar. Allegedly Rimmer would lure workers to his place after supper to work on building his cabins by lamplight. Over the course of a few years, he built quite a homestead on the site. This included two other log cabins, an icehouse, a caretaker log cabin and a large two-story red rolled-asphalt sided boathouse. The boathouse became a Canoe Lake landmark, marking the entranceway to Portage Bay as it was visible from way down the lake. Besides his government pension his main source of income was renting out his three cabins and half a dozen canoes to visiting fishermen and day tourists during the summer.

---

[80] Correspondence in the Ministry lease archives.

One of his most distinquished guests for several summers was the famous Group of Seven artist Lawren Harris whose son was attending Camp Ahmek. In 1936 the Department realized that he was running a limited commercial enterprise and issued him a proper commercial lease and land use permit.

Rimmer's bequest to Miss Webb seemed to have caused tremendous consternation on the part of the Department. It is unclear whether this was because she was an unmarried woman or because she was an unknown or both. An investigation was instigated, which included a detailed request to her lawyers for answers to what seemed to be quite personal questions. After two years of investigation of the relationship between Rimmer and Miss Webb, no "smoking guns" were ever found so she was finally issued a lease in 1941. She took over from Rimmer and ran her business happily for quite a number of years. The canoe rentals she continued until 1963 and the cabin rentals until she died in 1967. Upon her death the Ontario Parks Integration Board immediately issued a memo advising that the Department should acquire the Webb lease as quickly as possible. Apparently the Department of Health had issued a request that living conditions for the Portage Store staff be improved. It was decided that the best way to do so was to expropriate the Webb lease and turn the site into staff cabins. Webb died before the expropriation took place and her estate executors offered to surrender the lease in 1967. The Department felt that the sum Webb sought was unreasonable and later that year expropriated the property. All of the beautiful log cabins and the red boathouse were torn down and replaced with the current Portage Store staff cabin.

Chapter 3
The Potter Creek Community

The Potter Creek Community

It's been raining all day. The kids and I have been stuck in the cabin and are suffering from acute cabin fever. It's time to take a hike, even if we all get wet. I get everyone into their foul weather gear and head to the boat. After a few minutes of heavy bailing and arguing as to who will get to sit on the dry spots under the wet seat cushions, we set off for the north end of the lake and a hike into history. Twenty minutes later we round Wabeek Pointe and the wind suddenly drops. In front of us, stuck in a stump about 20 feet from the shore, is a brown sign with yellow lettering. An arrow to the right points the way to Joe Lake Dam and the main route north for interior canoe trippers. Another arrow pointing to the left directs us into Potter Creek. We are careful to avoid the sand bar that extends out into the channel. Over the last 100 years this little strip of sand has caused great injury to many an unsuspecting motorboat engine and canoe keel. Just up the western shore is the only flat open area on Canoe Lake. Most of it is now covered with scrub spruce trees as a result of a 1960s reforestation effort. It is hard to visualize the miles and miles of railroad siding that once existed on this spot. The first little cabin we see somehow seems out of place. If I think hard I can remember the original two-story cabin that graced this spot for more than 75 years. It was the "Souler House," one of the original Gilmour supply depot houses. Though likely originally whitewashed, as was the custom at the turn of the century, I knew it only as a dull, faded driftwood gray colour. The original house was taken down in the late '70s and parts of it were used to build the cabin that is on the site now. Nothing remains of the large vegetable garden that used to exist on the north end of the property.

A little farther down the western shore is an open meadow that reveals the remains of a tall stone chimney. Farther still are two more small cabins set near the shore. The gray remains of a broken down bridge that once joined the western and eastern shores of the creek lies in the distance. Close to the now empty point where the bridge must have reached the western shore is a stand of spruce trees surrounded by a circular collection of notched concrete blocks that looks mysteriously like a train turnstile. We tie our boat to the trees and survey the scene. Old photographs that I have tell me that we are standing on the remains of a sawdust burner. It fed a saw mill that had been built on this site in 1926 by wholesale lumber merchants A. E. Clark & Son of Toronto.

We walk across the open meadow and venture into the dark stand of spruce trees about 20 feet from shore. To our astonishment the forest reveals a two-story concrete shell. High above our heads we can see where the floor joists must have been anchored into the walls and lower down the huge holes where the logs must have been fed into the mill. It's hard to believe that this whole area was a bustling sawmill and that during its heyday, the entire creek that we just left would have been filled with logs. The logging venture wasn't profitable (likely due to the Depression) and the venture was closed down 10 years later. Unsightly piles of cut lumber still on the shoreline were of concern to the leaseholders when Joe Omanique relaunched the mill in the 1940s. His tugboats would tow huge log booms everyday up to the mill from Tea Lake and Smoke Creek. Loose logs were a major lake hazard to boats, canoes and landing floatplanes, especially at night.

Past the remains of the bridge, the creek narrows considerably and eventually passes under the old railway bed, now a lumber road. It eventually becomes impassable at a small set of rapids, which lead to Rainbow Lake to the north. Except for the three windswept cottages, nothing remains of the community that lived around the mills and the railroad. I try to imagine what the community must have been like for women like Mrs. Ratan, living in an environment dominated by gruff, hard-working lumber and railway men. But the mosquitoes are bad in this part of the creek and the kids pester me to go back to the open waters of Canoe Lake. I think about the families that called Potter Creek their year-round home long after the lumber mills, the railway station and the hotels had all disappeared.

Canoe Lake Mill on Potter Creek, 1926—
APMA #3935(top) and APMA #3934 (bottom)Wallace Penock

Omanique Lumber Mill, Early 1940s—APMA #5850 Helen Jones

Omanique Lumber Mill on Potter Creek
circa 1940s—APMA #1272 J. Leech-Porter

Panorama of Mill Site Looking West, circa 1940s—
APMA #5888 Chuck Matthews

Remains of Omanique Lumber Mill on Potter Creek
circa likely 1950s—APMA #1273 MNR

Aerial View of Potter Creek Canoe Lake Station to
Mill Site—APMA #5030 MNR

Steam Tug Boat Towing Cribs of Hardwood up
Canoe Lake, 1928/29—APMA #6258 George Garland/Dr. C. Chapple

Kate Stringer

Stringer Cabin
(formerly the "Souler House" on Potter Creek)—APMA #6063 Sandy Gage

Kate Stringer

In 1927 Kate and Jack Stringer (known as Mammy and Pappy) assumed the lease on the "Souler House." As indicated previously, the building had originally been part of the package bought by Dr. Pirie from the Gilmour receivers in 1905 and sold to a Mr. I. T. Insley. The Stringers were from Eganville where Jack had owned a barbershop. They had 16 children, a remarkable feat even in those days. They lost their home in a fire that destroyed much of Eganville, and moved to Killaloe to start over. Though Pappy loved barbering, (even after he retired he kept his barber's stool set up in a shed) he decided to become a Park ranger. In 1919 he joined his son Dan on the Algonquin Park ranger staff. Several years later Mammy joined him, staying both at Brulé Lake and Brent before settling on Potter's Creek. Jack had deep blue eyes (that his son Jimmy inherited) and thin white hair. Mammy was very easy going with a sweet innocence about her and was liked by everyone. She wasn't very tall, but had a unique style of her own. For some unknown reason, she always coloured her hair, loved to wear high-topped boots but refused ever to have her picture taken. By the late 1920s, most of the kids were off on their own and the whole family got together only on holidays. One main social activity each week was the Stringer get-togethers on Saturday nights to listen to whatever hockey or baseball game was playing on their old battery-powered radio.

The lake gossip was always awash with Stringer stories of one kind or another. Every Stringer was an excellent paddler, fisherperson and woodsperson. One good story had two of the Stringer brothers appearing at the Algonquin Hotel guide house and hearing that there was a dance at the Highland Inn. They had just returned from having spent a long two weeks guiding in the Park. At the news of the dance, they immediately jumped into a canoe with fresh clothes in a backpack. They paddled down through Canoe Lake, carried the canoe over the short portage into Smoke at the bottom of Portage Bay. From there they paddled and carried through Little Island, Beaver Pond, Tanamakoon and into Cache Lake. At Waubuno Island they changed clothes, went to the dance and kicked up their heels until the early morning hours. After many hours of dancing up a storm, they retraced their steps to Canoe Lake only to find a worried Mammy awake at dawn with breakfast waiting for them.[81]

---

[81] Story excerpted from the Cache Lake History, 1996.

Mammy must have been very capable, as another story had her swimming up the lake from the Portage Store landing with a cook stove on her back and a turkey cooking in the oven. A third story had her paddling to a dance at Camp Ahmek when she was 8 1/2 months pregnant, stopping on the shore when she went into labour, delivering her child by herself and then continuing on to dance until the wee hours of the morning. Mammy had a weak spot for one of her youngest sons, Jim. No matter how old he got, Mammy always referred to Jim as the baby of the family. Even when he was in his 60s she was heard to comment,

> "Now dear, watch out and don't get your feet wet my child."[82]

Like most of his brothers, Jim was a superb fisherman, especially fly-fishing and was very knowledgeable about local prime fishing holes. He was also an excellent cook and guide on a fishing trip. He was kind, warm-hearted and gentle and had tremendous artistic talent. He would sit and draw small postcards for hours. Though uneducated in a formal way he had lots of native intelligence and loved to talk. In later years he built a large vegetable garden on the property and would bring lettuce and carrots to leaseholders on the lake. He used to tell stories that nobody believed, but sounded exciting. One involved picking up an axe and chasing a wolf across the lake in winter, and catching it. Another included claiming the bounty for two wolves he found dead by the side of Highway 60 that had been struck and killed by two women driving by. One year at a Taylor Statten Camps September Camp cocktail party Jim was elected "Mayor of Canoe Lake" and was duly crowned with an official "Chain of Office" made of beer can rings.

Jimmy accidentally drowned in Canoe Lake in the spring of 1973. There are several accounts of his death, but the most credible story is Roy MacGregor's from his book "A Life in the Bush," with supplemental narrative from Lulu Gibson. Roy had been asked to write an article for MacLean's magazine about his family's connection to Tom Thomson, and thus had met Jimmy for a drink at the Empire Hotel in Huntsville. After a few hours full of tall tales and much laughter, Roy dropped him off at his room. The next morning Jimmy hitched a ride into the Park and began walking over the ice to the Stringer cabin, pulling groceries on a sleigh. It was an unseasonably warm February day and Jimmy never made it to the

---

[82] Notes from an interview with Marion Cherry Stringer, one of Kate's youngest daughters.

top end of Canoe Lake. When Jimmy didn't arrive as expected, his brother Wam got worried and started looking. He eventually found a hole in the ice, in which Jimmy's pipe pouch was floating. He had fallen through the ice almost at the precise point where Tom Thomson's body had been found more than 50 years earlier. His wrists were all cut from the ice, probably from when he was trying to pull himself out of the water. Wam felt responsible for what happened and guilty that he hadn't gone with Jimmy to Huntsville on that trip. It took him years to get over that. He used to say that every winter for years he could see that hole in the ice.[83]

Wam was a Canoe Lake legend and amongst other great skills had an amazing gift for music. Most instruments he could pick up and play instantly. He would play the fiddle and do the square-dance calling at the train station square dances. One of his lasting contributions to the culture on the lake was the creation of the Wam Stringer Memorial Square Dance Orchestra. It became one of the great sources of entertainment in the district. The group would play at square dances arranged at the various children's camps in the area, Arowhon Pines Resort or at the Algonquin Hotel. If needed they would borrow the piano from the Algonquin Hotel and drag it to each dance location. When the hotel was being taken down, one leaseholder bartered the piano for an old antique saddle rifle and moved it to his cabin where it still resides and is in use today.

Over the years, many of the Stringer children worked for the ministry in various capacities. Other than Wam and Jim, who took over the family lease in the '50s after Mammy and Pappy died, only Marion and Mabel, the youngest daughters, chose to settle on Canoe Lake. Marion was one of 17 pupils with Jean and Lulu Farley at the one-room Canoe Lake School in 1929. The girls decided to take out their own lease and were able to get one nearby. In an impulsive moment Pappy bought one of the old lumber company staff houses. He had a crazy idea that he and Mammy could move into it so that she would not have to manage such a large house. But Mammy wanted no part of it, saying that it was "too small for all of their stuff."[84] So he sold it to Mabel and Marion for $1 and had it moved to their site just up Potter Creek. In 1942 the sisters moved to Toronto to work in a war munitions plant, but in 1945 they returned to Canoe Lake to run the outfitting store at Joe Lake for George Merrydew. Mabel also worked for a couple of summers in the Wapomeo kitchen. Marion stills spends every summer at Canoe Lake and Mabel makes it up when she can.

---

[83] Interviews with Lulu and Gibby Gibson, by Don Standfield, 1992.
[84] Interview with Marion Stringer Cherry, 1999.

Recently, with the help of Mabel and Marion, Mary Colson Clare and Eleanor Wright were able to finally establish the list of children in birth order including: John (known as Jake), William (known as Bill), Lila, Daniel (known as Dan or Mud), Cyril, James (known as Jim), Earl (known as Boliver), Albert (known as Bert), Wilmer (known as Wam), Catherine (known as Katie who married Russ Ullman), Dellas (known as Dellie), Stella (known as Moon who married Aubrey Dunne), Omer (known as Bung), Mabel, Roy and finally Marion.

Painting of Stringer Cabin by Irma Manning, circa 1960s
Hanging on the Manning Cabin Wall—Clemson Collection

Top Row: Jean Farley, Mammy Stringer, Pappy Stringer,
Marion Stringer Cherry. Bottom Row: Mabel Stringer Cooke,
Leila Stringer Grenke, Lulu Farley Gibson—Bullock Collection

Lulu Farley Gibson

Lulu Farley Gibson and Gibby Gibson in "Jazzy,"
circa 1940s—Karen Farley Bullock

Lulu Farley Gibson

Lulu Farley Gibson first came to Ålgonquin Park with her parents Margaret and Everett Farley in 1931. Her father had been appointed lumber
foreman for the Canoe Lake Lumber Company. Living in Oshawa, Everett
was fearful of being laid off, so Canoe Lake seemed like a good career
move. He packed up his wife Margaret and daughter Lulu, jumped on the
train and settled the family north of the Stringers on Potter Creek. There
he built a beautiful split-level cabin out of cut logs with a hardwood floor
inside. He installed a three-piece bath, which was unheard of at the time,
and had built a beautiful big stone fireplace. Later a boathouse and two
sheds were added. One shed was used as a stable where he kept three horses
and a cow. The horses were always being used to haul timber or ice that
Farley would cut in the winter months for camps and cottagers. Sometimes he would hitch them to his sleigh and take everyone on rides across
the snow.

Over the years everyone on the lake grew to depend upon the Farleys.
Everett would open existing cottages in the spring, close them up in the
fall and make whatever repairs were wanted or needed. He would build
cabins for new arrivals and add additions, porches or sleeping bunkees to
accommodate growing lake families. For a time he used to look after the
level of the lakes at Tea Lake Dam for Ontario Hydro. He started a water
taxi service with his huge inboard cedar strip motorboat, called "Jazzy,"
which chugged up the lake and could be heard for miles. When "Jazzy"
retired he bought a white launch, called it "Tyree" and used it for many
years. Residents would write or in later years telephone and he would pick
up folks and their belongings at the train station or at the Portage Store
and take them to their cabins. Even after Highway 60 was built, folks
would phone from Huntsville and ask that he meet them at the leaseholders' dock. He was always there waiting in his boat to take them across to
their cabins. In what eventually became a local tradition, he would help
unload their gear, sit awhile and make conversation. Then, not wishing to
be rude, he would join the new arrivals for a quick celebratory drink before
chugging off down the lake. One pair of newlyweds who settled at the
south end of Canoe Lake in 1946 fondly recall the year that Everett delivered to them a new double bed and mattress. They were spread precari-
ously between two canoes and towed down the lake behind his old boat.[85]

---

[85] *Gertrude Baskerville–The Lady of Algonquin Park*, by author, pg. 35.

In April 1936, Robert Pinchin, who had been the chief clerk of the Canoe Lake Lumber Company and secretary of the local Canoe Lake school, resigned his job as postmaster and Everett took over the job. Margaret and Lulu became his chief assistants and handled all of the mail for the railway workers and their families, the local cottagers and businesses, and what remained of the lumber camp operations. In summer this included mail for all the local children's camps (Camp Ahmek and Camp Wapomeo on Canoe Lake, Camp Arowhon farther north on Teepee Lake and Camp Tamakwa on Tea Lake). It was hard to believe the number of letters that would go in and out from all the camps all summer long. Back then it cost 4 cents to mail a letter and 10 cents to register one. A little later the Farleys had another daughter, Jean, who was born on Canoe Lake under the watchful eye of Molly Colson. Jean attended the Canoe Lake Elementary School and then went on to attend St. Joseph's Catholic School in North Bay and business college in Orillia. She eventually married and settled in Huntsville.

Lulu Farley had blue eyes, a warm smile, and a gentle manner. Her wavy hair was pulled back in a way that displayed a unique look of tremendous strength of character.[86] In summer Lulu would take the Smoke Lake mail to the Portage Store, chugging down the lake in a wooden boat. Sometimes she would take the long way around through Bonita Narrows and Smoke Creek and deliver it directly to the float plane hangar on the north end of Smoke Lake. In winter she would use a horse and cutter or dog team to go down to Smoke Lake to pick up the bags of mail and bring them back to the post office to be sorted and picked up by local residents. Depending on the weather and ice conditions Lulu would travel on the lakes or use the winter roads that were kept open by the lumber companies. She had several sled dogs, (Mikey her favourite, Belto and Togo) who loved to pull her dog sled.

In 1945 Lulu Farley married Gibby Gibson, took out a lease and together they built a cabin just down the shore from her parent's cabin. She had met Gibby a few years earlier when he was in the Park as part of the road crew building Highway 60. Gibby was a short, well-built man with arms that look like they belong to Popeye.[87] His eyes would give the impression that they were forever laughing and his high cheekbones were always rosy in

[86]Stories excerpted from an interview with Lulu and Gibby Gibson, by Don Standfield, 1992.
[87]Stories and descriptions excerpted from an interview with Lulu and Gibby Gibson, by Don Standfield, 1992.

colour. His mouth was constantly supplying the room with smart comments. He was quite musical and had an accordion that he used to play. He earned 25 cents a day, which included a change of clothes, some tobacco and a roof over his head. When the road was finished, he decided to stay on and boarded with the Farleys until he went overseas during World War II. Lulu and Jean's mother Margaret, the uncomplaining ever-loyal helpmate, died in 1949 and several years later Everett remarried. According to the local gossip, Lulu didn't approve of the new Mrs. Betty Farley. She resigned her position as assistant postmistress and severed all ties to her father. Allegedly she never spoke to her father again in his life, even though their cabins were next door to each other. Everett died in 1971 and his loss was a great blow to the community. He was considered by most to be a "Man Amongst Men."[88]

Betty wasn't well enough to stay on Potter Creek by herself all year round, so she moved to a home for the elderly in Gananoque where she died in 1974. The Ministry expropriated the property in 1973 and, as per policy for expropriated buildings, burned the lovely Farley cabin to the ground soon after. As a memorial the huge stone fireplace still stands by the shore-line.

Lulu needed to work so she joined the Camp Ahmek staff and was responsible for all of the nightly baking . Her services were in high demand for the treats that she would prepare for the hundreds of boys that wouldn't eat their main courses at dinner, but would wolf down the desserts. Gibby worked at probably every possible job known to have existed on Canoe Lake. He was always busy fixing camp generators and was well known for magically breathing life into an old outboard engine that was close to being tossed out by a cottager. One year he rescued the Thompsons' engine that had fallen into Bonita Narrows. He went diving for it and after a few tries was able to bring it up from the bottom. He dried it out and to everyone's relief got it running again.

According to Lulu, one winter Gibby had arrived at the Portage Store after hitching a ride in from Huntsville with a couple of arms full of groceries. He was tired and didn't want to walk all the way to Potter Creek on the ice so he borrowed a car that was just sitting there at Portage Store . It was a late '30s Buick, with a spark advance that made it easy to jump-start.

---

[88]Comments in the minutes of the 1971 Canoe Lake Leaseholders Association.

He put planks down so that he could get it from the shore of the lake onto the ice. The ice was flexing under the weight of the car and was just thick enough to hold him up as long as he kept the car moving. He decided to remain standing on the running board just in case it went through the ice. Just past Little Wapomeo Island, the engine started to overheat and there was steam pouring out from every little crack in the hood. The neighbours up on Potter Creek heard him coming and were standing out on the shore watching as he came around Wabeek Pointe. They all scattered when he drove the car right up onto the shore next to the house.

After that experience there was no way he was going to take it out onto the ice again, so the only way to get it back to the Portage Store was via the railway tracks. One of his part time jobs was to light the fire in the Canoe Lake Station and make sure the clock was working before the train came. Because of this he knew the train schedules and when it was likely to be safe to take the car back to the store on the railway tracks. The tires didn't fit the rails exactly but he and Lulu headed off anyway, bumping all the way to Cache Lake. Highway 60, it turned out, wasn't that much better for bumps than the railroad tracks, but hey did return that Buick safe and sound to the Portage Store parking lot and the owner never realized where that old car had been.[89]

Being such a character, Gibby was always off on some wild adventure or another while Lulu would anxiously keep the home fires burning. One winter Gibby thought he could make some quick money by taking on the job of hauling a huge smokestack for one of the lumber camps up to Burnt Island Lake. He figured that he could get it up and back pretty quickly. He hitched up Lulu's dog team to a large sled, tied on the smokestack and headed out. Unfortunately the weather conditions weren't the greatest. The snow was terribly soft, so the stack wouldn't stay on the sled. Instead of the quick dash to the lumber camp, it took over 18 hours to get there. He fed the dogs on the way up, but didn't have anything for himself. When he arrived everyone was asleep and he had to wake up the cook to get something to eat and see where he could stay for the night. He ate a bit of the left over dinner, gave the dogs some scraps and bones and went to sleep in one of the empty horse stalls for the night. The next morning he headed back to Canoe Lake and arrived late in the afternoon. As he said later, it wasn't one of his most profitable ideas.[90]

---

[89]Excerpted from an interview with Lulu and Gibby Gibson, by Don Standfield, 1992.
[90]Excerpted from an interview with Lulu and Gibby Gibson, by Don Standfield, 1992.

In his later years, Gibby was a night watchman at Camp Ahmek and would also help out from time to time in the Ahmek kitchen. Gibby had circulation problems, which led to several amputations on one leg. First he lost his toe, then his heel and then everything below the knee. But he never let this disability slow him down. Sue Ebbs, the daughter of Adele Statten Ebbs, remembers one winter when she was up at Little Wap with a dozen or so of her friends. They saw Gibby flying up the lake on a snowmobile dressed in a huge bear skin coat wearing pajamas and a slipper on his one remaining leg. A few years later these same circulation problems started in his other leg. Rather than go through the same process again, he had the doctors amputate the entire leg below the knee. Eventually living on Potter Creek year round became too difficult so Gibby and Lulu Gibson would spend the winters in Parry Sound. At Christmas in 1992, Gibby passed away as did Lulu the following September.[91]

Lulu Farley (left), Margaret Farley (right),
Jean Farley (seated)

---

[91]After Lulu's death her niece took over the Gibson lease.

Lulu Farley and Dog Team Delivering the Mail, 1944—
APMA #6176 Chuck Gray

Canoe Lake Post Office, 1940—APMA #5853 Helen Jones

Farley Cottage, 1974—APMA #2597 MNR

Everett Farley (left) with Bill Reid—Loyst Collection

Betty Farley—Loyst Collection

Margaret Farley—Bullock Collection

Gibby Gibson in Later Years—
Bullock Collection

Lulu Farley "Dressed to Kill" as a Young Girl—
Bullock Collection

Lulu Farley with her Sled Dog, circa 1940s—
Bullock Collection

Chapter 4
The Leaders

Chapter 4
The Leaders

Sue Ebbs, whom we all call Swebbs, has invited us over to Little Wap for lunch so that she and I can visit and my twins can play with her two grandchildren who are about the same age. Swebbs comes from a long line of strong women. Her grandmother was Ethel Statten, known to us all as Tonakela. It was she, with the support of her husband, Taylor Statten, who started Camp Wapomeo in 1924 and ran it for decades. Adele Ebbs, better known as Couchie, is Swebb's mother. Couchie spent her entire working life running Camp Wapomeo from the early 1930s until 1975. From where I stand outside of Couchie's cabin, I can hear all the kids squawking and giggling with the babysitter down by the south point. From here they can easily walk into the water, but it's a different sort of swimming experience than jumping off the dock at our cabin. Here the bottom is not sandy, as it is over at Camp Ahmek or at Ridpath's beach. It's the kind of silty mud that squishes between your toes. It's also strewn with rocks and sticks, so you have to place your foot down carefully at each step. I look across the lake. The north end of Big Wapomeo Island is clearly visible from where we sit. A screen door slams and two young girls race out of their cabin in the direction of the dining hall for lunch.

I open Couchie's cabin door and walk through the back kitchen into the main room. Her aura and that of her mother, Tonakela, is so powerful that I am overwhelmed and grab the doorframe for support. I take a deep breath and the moment passes. I take a step or two into the room. The main part of the cabin is made out of square cut logs. Each was magically fitted together by a master craftsman, Charlie Musclow, brother of Gertie Baskerville.[92] The walls are covered with pictures, paintings, and illustrated paddle blades of times and people gone past. The huge stone fireplace is black with soot. Grouped around it is a small coffee table carved out of wood, several couches and two big armchairs reminiscent of a different age. Every space is covered with books, handmade crafts and Indian artifacts of every shape, size and type. On one corner table rests a bouquet of tree branches, each branch with different bird's nest resting on it.[93] In another corner is a double bed covered with a beautiful red

---

[92]For more details about Gertie and Charlie, see *Gertrude Baskerville–The Lady of Algonquin Park.*
[93]Notes from an interview with Adele Ebbs, by Don Standfield, 1991.

Hudson Bay blanket, its glorious black stripes providing a stark symmetry. It's hard to believe that this cabin is more than 60 years old. It's even harder to believe that The Chief and Tonakela's cabin, just up the worn path a short way, is over 85 years old. What a legacy and influence these two women have brought to Canoe Lake and to countless numbers of other women and young girls during the last 77 years. The noontime grace starts up from the Camp Wapomeo dining hall and I can hear the sweet voices straining hard to reach the high notes.

> *Thankful for life and all the joys of living,*
> *For food and friend and Nature's bounteous giving,*
> *We take our stand with free men everywhere,*
> *Who spend their lives to make earth still more fair,*
> *And spread life's noblest gifts that all may share.*[94]

My memories of camp life both as a longtime camper and as a staff member come rushing to me. Like most kids, I loved the swimming and the sailing, horseback riding and tennis, the camp plays and musical events and the arts and crafts programs for rainy days. But even now, after nearly 30 years, I am unable to explain in a coherent way what it felt like to experience a Camp Wapomeo canoe trip. The skills I learned with five other girls my own age, such as packing, carrying huge pack sacks over long portages, paddling until I felt that my arms would fall off, setting up and breaking down a campsite, were unique. The self confidence that grew as I mastered chopping wood properly with an axe, lighting fires with no more than two matches regardless of the weather or condition of the wood, cooking meals over an open fire, carrying a canoe single-handed and controlling my fear when alone in the woods has helped me immeasurably my whole life. Couchie and Tonakela, as female role models at a time when there weren't very many, taught us so much about ourselves and what was important in life – comradeship, simple food, a warm place to sleep at night and lots of laughter. More importantly the experience taught us that it was alright to be strong and capable and independent. Swebbs comes up behind me and hands me a cup of tea. We sit down in her comfy armchairs and she begins her family's story.

---

[94] Words by Dr. A.E. Haydon and Music by Bill Scott, 1948.

Ethel (Tonakela) Statten and Adele (Couchie) Statten Ebbs

Ethel (Tonakela) Statten and Adele (Couchie) Statten Ebbs

Ethel Statten had met and married Taylor Statten in Toronto in 1906. At the time Statten held the position of Boys Work Secretary with the YMCA and was heavily involved at a training camp at Geneva Park on Lake Couchiching. He was also strongly influenced by Ernest Thompson Seton and his Woodcraft League of America, later adopting many of their principles at Camp Ahmek, which he established on the shores of Canoe Lake in 1921. Ethel's first experience of Canoe Lake was during the winter of 1912. The Stattens and a group of friends decided to take a trip to Algonquin Park, which was a common winter vacation spot at the time. They took the train to the Highland Inn on Cache Lake and from there decided to snowshoe the nine miles into Canoe Lake. Dressed in a full-length skirt, crinoline and presumably long johns, she headed out with the group along the snow-covered train tracks heading west. They ate a chilly lunch on the verandah of one of the Gilmour Island cottages. Following the shoreline to the north took them past a lovely little island located just south of the Mowat Post Office. After warming up with a cup of tea shared with the postmaster they went on to Canoe Lake Station and caught the train back to the Highland Inn.[95]

The next summer Taylor, who had been given the nickname "The Chief," came up on another exploratory trip to Canoe Lake and camped on the north end of what later was named Big Wapomeo Island. Statten again saw the lovely little island to the north, successfully leased it and later named it Little Wapomeo Island. Because of the nature of his work at the YMCA, the Stattens were only able to get away to their island hideaway in September after the YMCA camping season. For the first few years they lived in a large teepee as Taylor wanted to experience what it might have been like to live like the Indians. Ethel was a very ardent outdoors person and very capable when it came to adapting and living outside in a teepee. She loved the Park as much as Taylor and according to his eldest daughter Adèle (nicknamed Couchie after Lake Couchiching):

"He was very lucky to have a wife who was such a sport."[96]

---

[95]Excerpted from C.A.M. Edwards biography of Taylor Statten and interviews with Sue Ebbs.
[96]Interview with Adele Ebbs, by Don Standfield, found in the Ministry archives.

Ethel soon abandoned her long dresses and adopted men's clothing, including high topped lace-up boots, long pants and work shirts, which was a much more convenient wardrobe.

Their teepee had a fire pit in the middle of the floor that when lit would send smoke out of the flaps at the top. Next to it was a kitchen area that was underneath a canvas tarpaulin. Here they would cook and eat outside on handmade birchbark furniture if the weather was fair. If the weather was bad, they would all sit around the fire inside the teepee. In 1916 they decided that it was now time to build a cabin. Folklore has it that Tom Thomson helped to clear the trees and brush from the island and hauled sand from Sim's Pit to mix with the cement for the beautiful stone fireplace. A prophetic inscription, which is still there today, was carved onto the wooden mantelpiece:

"Here let the northwoods spirit kindle fires of friendship."

Often the family, which now included Taylor Jr. born in 1915 and Page born in 1918, would paddle to Crown Lake or to Ragged Lake to catch strings of trout. They would stay overnight in an old lumber cabin that was along the way. Since it was fall, it was often so cold that their hands would freeze in their mittens and they would return with them completely covered in ice. One marvelous story that Couchie tells of this time involved an invitation that she, Bill Hayhurst and Mary Northway had received when she was about 19 years old. Her father and a guide, Ed Ryan had invited the younger ones to join a deer hunting party.[97] The plan was to run the deer through a portage. The girls were to shoot them as they passed by. It was cold that day and after awhile Adele and Mary got tired of waiting and were playing leapfrog to keep warm. Suddenly they heard the howls of the hounds and realized that their guns were way down the portage. They never got to them in time, but did see all the beautiful deer come bounding down the portage. They lost their reputations as hunters and were never invited back again with the men. However as Couchie admitted later, she wasn't all that interested in shooting deer so was never bothered much that she wasn't asked back.[98]

In the summer of 1921, Statten launched Camp Ahmek on Canoe Lake in a protected bay with an extensive sandy beach on the northeastern shore. It

---

[97] Excerpted from an interview with Adele Ebbs, by Don Standfield, 1991, found in the Ministry archives.

[98] Interview with Adele Ebbs, by Don Standfield, found in the Ministry archives.

was the first Canadian-owned private camp in Algonquin Park. Statten had obtained a "license of occupation" for five acres for a boys camp and launched an initial six-week woodcraft program for 60 campers.[99] Statten took on the Ojibwa Indian name "Gitchiahmek," meaning "Great Beaver," and Ethel took on the name "Tonakela," meaning "You First." Though not directly involved, Tonakela was a strong behind-the-scenes advisor. One interesting need of those early years, likely endorsed strongly by her, was a request in 1923 to the Department to bring five cows into the Park for the summer to provide fresh milk for the campers.

In 1924 the Stattens decided that they would launch a girls' camp as well. The original plan was to build on a site that they had investigated on Tea Lake. But after some consideration and major objections by Tonakela to being so far away from Camp Ahmek, they decided that it would make much better sense to house Camp Wapomeo close by. There was great controversy at the time as many critics felt that it was totally inappropriate for boys and girls to be so close to each other. Nevertheless Camp Wapomeo was started on Little Wapomeo Island with 60 campers attending its first summer session. Tonakela learned about directing a camp from "The Chief." She hired top leaders with training and practical experience in youth leadership.[100] She was a courageous, no-nonsense policy setter and maintained direct supervision of the operation with, as was recalled by a staff member many years later, "a steel fist embedded in a rabbit fur glove."[101]

By 1927 there were more than 100 campers enrolled at Camp Wapomeo and it was clear that the camp would have to expand. The Stattens' preference was to move the camp to Big Wapomeo Island, which had been leased that year by a Statten relative. At the time there was significant controversy as this island was the only good location for campsites mid-lake on what was even then a main canoe route to the north. Eventually it was decided that the park rangers would solve the problem by building a number of other campsites on the lake. Unfortunately Popcorn Island became a campsite, though perhaps an unofficial one, and within a few years was nearly denuded of trees. In 1928, the older campers were moved to Big Wapomeo Island and a new dining hall was built. The senior girls would only join the younger ones for council rings and two handsome war canoes that could accommododate more than 20 people were used to transport everyone to both the islands and to Ahmek.

---

[99] Over the years as the camp grew, additional land was leased and added to the core site so that the camp now stretches all along the bay from Ghost Walk Creek almost to Windy Isle.
[100] *Fires of Friendship: Eighty Years of the Taylor Statten Camps*, pgs. 32-33.
[101] Ibid, pgs. 32-33.

Tonakela had several good friends who eventually made Canoe Lake their summer homes. One was Alice Matthews. Her husband Chuck was a partner with J.E. Sampson. Their firm, Sampson and Matthews, designers and lithographers, produced all types of graphic documents from annual reports to brochures. Chuck loved the bush and cared greatly about the well being of the Park. In 1973 he received the "Order of Canada" for his dedication to the country. Chuck's first visit to Canoe Lake was on a fishing trip in 1921. He came in by train and on the way home through Canoe Lake Station, Taylor Statten boarded the train and sat with him. During the leg to Scotia Junction and on to Huntsville they struck up a deep and long-lasting friendship. Each summer for years, the Matthews would visit the Stattens at Little Wapomeo. Their friendship was so close that in 1927 "The Chief" added a cabin, for their exclusive use on Little Wap. Through Statten, Chuck also became good friends with Park Superintendent Frank MacDougall. At least once he went flying with MacDougall on one of his air inspections of the Park.

Eventually the Matthews family grew, and they decided to take out their own lease at the south end of Canoe Lake. With Alice's help, in the fall of 1940, Chuck chose a site on the west side because he wanted to see Camp Ahmek and considered the east shore to be too hot. The channel between Gilmour Island and Camp Wapomeo gave him a clear view of the Ahmek waterfront. During that first winter after the issue of their lease, they built a scale model of their dream cottage using toy logs and cardboard. This was added to and altered many times during the course of the winter and by late spring plans had been finalized sufficiently to commence building.

In the spring of 1941 Chuck contacted Charlie Musclow who had done such a great job building Couchie's cabin on Little Wap a few years previously. Charlie unfortunately was not interested in building it for him. He had made little profit on the last few and flatly stated that he was not going to build any more cottages. After some contemplation, Chuck decided to make Charlie a proposition that would guarantee him a profit. As Chuck told Charlie, "I'll pay you 10 percent above all of your material and wage cost, you can keep the books. I'll respect them and pay you 10 percent over your cost. On that basis Charlie built our cabin and did a very satisfactory job."[102]

---

[102] Interview with Chuck Matthews, by Rory MacKay, 1975.

Charlie Musclow was a very special craftsman. He cut white spruce logs in the spring at Sim's Pit, peeled them in June and transported them down Canoe Lake by water. He then cleared the site by removing a number of large hemlock and yellow birch trees, and hence the name of the cottage became "Tall Timbers." The logs were cut by hand into 18- to 20-foot lengths with a sharp axe, shaving the joints until they fit perfectly. The fireplace was designed by J.E. Sampson and constructed by McKinney Brothers of Huntsville, who had also built the fireplaces for Camp Ahmek and Frank Braucht. The cabin was ready for occupancy late in the 1941 season. Over the succeeding years, additional cabins were built for the Matthews children, one of whom obtained a lease on the adjacent property to the south. One was built out of square logs sawn in half that had been obtained from a barn in Madawaska, originally part of the J. R. Booth estate. Through Chuck's work and his membership in the "Arts and Letters Club," Alice and Chuck became friends with Group of Seven artists A. Y. Jackson and A.J. Casson, who would visit frequently. This solidified Canoe Lake's position as a center of artistic activity long after the passing of Tom Thomson.

Other dear friends of Tonakela and The Chief were Elsie Ridpath and her husband Jack. Elsie was born in England in 1900 and came to Canada as a young girl. She had met Tonakela in Toronto and was brought up to camp to run the mailroom at Camp Wapomeo for several summers. There she met and married Jack Ridpath. Jack was born about 1885 in Lakefield, Ontario, into a family of six boys and three girls. As a young boy, he played in the woods and along the logging waterfronts in the Haliburton area. At age 10 he was put in a total cast to repair hip damage and took up carving to pass the time. By age 14 he was now a skilled carver, so his family brought him to Toronto to carve for Rawlinson's Furniture on Yonge Street. By age 20 he was on his own, establishing first The Cabinet Shop and then Ridpath's Limited. Through the Arts and Letters Club he met Chuck Matthews and Taylor Statten. He came to Algonquin Park with Taylor Statten before 1920 to select a site for Camp Ahmek and throughout the 1920s and '30s he would carve furniture and totem poles for Ahmek including the Tom Thomson Totem Pole in 1930.

In 1949, the Ridpaths decided to take out their own lease just north of their dear friends the Matthews. On the site they also built a beautiful square-cut log cabin using the same J.R. Booth estate logs as the Matthews.

In the 1950s Jack started the "Chiselers Club." He would hold weekly carving classes for those on the lake interested in learning how to carve. Many of the fruits of these carving efforts can still be seen at leaseholder cabins throughout the area. At one is a coffee table with a bear carved in it. At another is a log wall with bear carvings and a wooden fire screen with a prayer inscribed.

Prayer of the Woods:
"I am the heat of your hearth on cold winter nights, the friendly shade screening you from the summer sun and my fruits are refreshing draughts quenching your thirst as you journey on. I am the beam that holds your house, the board of your table, the bed on which you lie and the timber that holds your boat. I am the handle of your hoe, the door of your homestead, the wood of your cradle and the shell of your coffin. I am the bread of kindness and the flower of beauty. Ye who pass by, listen to my prayer: harm me not."

Jack died suddenly of a heart attack while visiting England in 1957. But Elsie continued to come to Canoe Lake every summer with her two children until she was no longer able. For many years she was an active member and hostess for Canoe Lake Leaseholder Association meetings, held each summer at one or another cabin. The friendly competitions as to whom could serve the most elegant lunch every year was a topic of much comment by many of the leaseholders at the time. In her later years, Elsie became best buddies with several other women on the lake. They would fish together hour after hour near Popcorn Island and discuss who on the lake was helping themselves to her ferns that graced the front walkway to her cabin. In 1990 Elsie Ridpath passed away and her children took over the Ridpath lease.

Given the close proximity of the boys' and girls' camps (about a mile of open water), one challenging task for Ethel and The Chief was to control inter-camp fraternizing. Often after dark, the older boys would take canoes from Camp Ahmek and set off to visit the girls at Camp Wapomeo. According to C.A.M. Edwards, The Chief (with Tonakela's tacit approval) would try to interrupt these dalliances by taking evening cruises on the lake in his powerboat, called the "ZaraGanza" after a nightclub in Havana.

He would discover a couple in a canoe, pull up to it swiftly, turn on the strong headlight and roar off again. This served to keep even the most ardent young people in check. On one occasion some clandestine meetings had been pre-arranged and the girls were awaiting the arrival of the boys. The Chief heard about it and went into action. He swiftly upset all the boys' canoes with the wake from his boat and effectively put a wet blanket on what might have been a very pleasant but forbidden evening for the young people.[103]

Later, Tonakela would help with the occasional patrols in her own boat, which she called the "Okeechobee." It was named after a lake in Florida they visited frequently during the winter. It was a cumbersome boat and only she could drive and land it well. If someone else offered to drive she would acquiesce to be polite, and then would sit in the back of the boat and instruct the driver on the correct way to drive for the entire length of the journey. One summer she and Elsie were cruising around the lake when the engine caught on fire. Elsie who couldn't swim, jumped into the water, so Tonakela had to jump in to save her.

By the late 1920s, Couchie was heavily involved with the management of Camp Wapomeo. Her future husband, Harry Ebbs, had arrived at Camp Ahmek as a counselor in training at about that same time. After their marriage Couchie and Dr. Harry decided to settle on the south end of Little Wapomeo Island. As mentioned previously, they had Gertrude Baskerville's brother, Charlie Musclow, build them a log cabin in 1937.[104] Couchie took over as director of Camp Wapomeo in 1930. Because of her interest in physical education and child development, she earned a degree at the University of Toronto and a teaching credential at the Ontario College of Education. This led to a stint as a physical education teacher at Oakwood Collegiate in the early '30s.[105] Couchie believed that camp directing was a profession in the field of education and she strove to attract top child development educators to spend time at Wapomeo with campers and staff.

During her years as the leader of Camp Wapomeo, Couchie felt very strongly that learning how to swim, paddle a canoe and sail a boat were important aspects of the camping experience. However, she also felt that camping was

---

[103]Excerpted from C.A.M. Edwards biography of Taylor Statten.
[104]See *Gertrude Baskerville—The Lady of Algonquin Park* for details of Charlie Musclow's time in Algonquin Park.
[105]*Fires of Friendship: Eighty Years of the Taylor Statten Camps*, pg. 29.

an opportunity for young people to learn how to share, cooperate and cope with all types of people, in all types of situations. Though she was kind, thoughtful, possessed of great amounts of common sense, she "did not suffer fools and had no patience for staff who didn't pull their share of the load."[106] This meant that sometimes people were quite afraid of her "look."

For many girls, going to camp was also the first time that they had been separated from their parents for any length of time. The independence and sense of teamwork that was learned was for most invaluable. As Couchie often said in speeches to camping associations around the world:

> "There is a new type of education that our children are going to need – physical fitness, good food, fresh air, hard physical work, opportunities for adventure, for pioneering. There should be chances for young people to strike out on their own, to have the thrill of exploring. Some of the adventures should be rigorous and take courage, only in this way can the feeling of independence be experienced. It is never too early for young women to learn to stand on their own feet and accept the consequences of their own behaviour."[107]

One of the lasting contributions that Taylor and Ethel made on Little Wapomeo Island was the garden in which they laboured in the spring and fall. It was a spectacular picture of glorious colours and a huge variety of flowers that ran from the lake up the stone steps to their cabin. One story told was that in order to keep the peace, the pair decided that Ethel would work starting at one end and The Chief would start at the other end so that each could have their own space. In the late fall of 1956, after an afternoon of garden work, Taylor Statten decided to take a rest before their evening meal. He died in his sleep. It was a great shock to everyone as he had been in excellent health and was only 68 years old. Chuck Matthews, a very close friend for more than 30 years, described Statten this way:

> "The most noteworthy man that was ever on Canoe Lake. He was an educator, humanitarian and great storyteller. His influence on thousands of young people was above reproach."[108]

---

[106]Ibid, pg. 70.
[107]Ibid, pg. 70.
[108]Interview with Chuck Matthews, by Rory MacKay, November 1975.

Tonakela stayed very active with Camp Wapomeo despite some ongoing medical problems. Even in her late 70s after she had a leg amputated due to a circulation problem, she still insisted on coming to camp every day to sit and visit with campers down by the waterfront. A special cabin was built for her so that she could rest there whenever she needed. She had a lifelong interest in weaving. Every spring she would thread all of the looms in the Weavery arts and crafts cabin at Camp Wapomeo. She passed away in 1969 just before her 87th birthday.

In 1975 Couchie and Dr. Harry decided to retire from the day-to-day management of Wapomeo. Couchie continued to stay involved with the American, Canadian and Ontario Camping Associations and in 1976 she was elected as an Honorary Life Associate of the Ontario Camping Association. In 1990 she received on behalf of all the Algonquin children's camps the Friends of Algonquin Park Directors Award in recognition of her contribution to camping in the Park.[109] Today, Couchie lives in Toronto with her son and tries to spend a part of every summer at her lovely cabin on Little Wapomeo Island.

Newly Built Couchie's Cabin, circa 1930s—
MNR Lease Archives

[109] *Fires of Friendship: Eighty Years of the Taylor Statten Camps*, pg. 199.

Tonakela and The Chief—
APMA #2382 Mervin Dupuis

Couchie, 1946—
APMA #4053 Mary Northway

Tonakela, Taylor II, Couchie at
Joe Lake Dam, 1920—Ebbs Collection

Couchie (Adele Statten Ebbs)—
Ebbs Collection

Tonakela (Ethel Statten)
in Front of "Okeechobee"—Ebbs Collection

Gathering at Nominegan Lodge on Smoke Lake, 1938
(left to right) Tonakela, The Chief, Gar Northway, Grannie, Flora
Morrison, Couchie, Taylor Statten II, Molly Colson, Alice Turner, Harry
Ebbs, Dottie—APMA #3417

Family Gathering at Little Wap, 1930
Right Rear: Tonakela, the Chief, Top Step Center—Couchie—APMA #7012

Jack and Elsie Ridpath with Children Joan and John,
circa 1940s—Yule Collection

Alice and Chuck Matthews Cabin, circa 1940s—Matthews Collection

Wood Carvings on Walls of Ridpath Cabin, 2000—
Clemson Collection

Tom Thomson Totem Pole and Cairn, circa 1940s—
Matthews Collection

Chapter 5
The Early Feminists

The Early Feminists

I've just come back from a visit with an old lake friend from childhood. These days we don't see each other much, but for many summers as kids we used to hang out together on Canoe Lake. Today she's one of the few women who are still able to spend most of the summer on Canoe Lake. Most others can visit only for weekends and the occasional vacation week or two. The environment around us and our lifestyle has really changed. The forests have aged and grown tall and stout, as have we. We all have electricity, running water, and telephones. Some even have satellite TV reception and VCRs, though they only admit it under duress. In the early '50s when most of our parents took up leases, there weren't any of these kinds of conveniences. Sometimes I do wonder how our mothers ever did it. They were not for the most part, camp-trained and hardy. They all would come and essentially stay by themselves all summer long, from the end of June until Labour Day. As my neighbour Mary Percival once said,

> *"We were gems-of-all-trades, not Jacks-of-all-trades. We coped alone. Did every job and fixed every problem with no help most of the time. It took ingenuity, that's what it took, courage and ingenuity!"*

Our fathers would come up and visit on the weekends, bringing with them weekly rations of fresh fruits and vegetables, which were heartily welcomed. Since the closest full service grocery store was the Huntsville I.G.A., a good 60 kilometers away, anything forgotten was usually done without. Once phone service was available, guests learned to always call from Huntsville on their way up to ask if anything was needed. Dwight had a wonderful old "Red and White" grocery store that had the greatest black balls in the world. Black balls were these hard, jaw-breaking candies full of wondrous colours and flavours that only appeared as it melted in the mouth. They were called black balls because the outside was black, which in addition to making the inside of one's mouth entirely black, also unfortunately made one's hands and anything one touched black as well. I think about those days and realize that it isn't likely that my kids will be able to experience Canoe Lake the same way that I did. Two months with nothing to do but swim, canoe and sail, explore the woods and let our imaginations run wild.

Wildlife isn't as prevalent as it once was. We never see deer and only the occasional moose or beaver. In some years there aren't even very many chipmunks or squirrels. We haven't seen a bear in these parts for over 20 years and though a few outhouses exist, most folks are switching over to self-composting systems. For me bears and outhouses will forever be intertwined. It's a result of a terrifying experience that I had as a kid, which still haunts me from time to time when I am up here alone. One evening, when I was about 10 years old, I decided to be very brave and went out to the outhouse by myself. Our outhouse is located about 50 feet away from the main cabin, set back in the woods. There I was, sitting on the throne, enjoying the sunset, when a huge black bear came waltzing through the clearing between the outhouse and the main cabin. I could see my mom standing at the cabin window with her hand over her mouth. I was so frightened that I couldn't scream. The bear, however, didn't notice me at all, but did notice the nearby tent. He wandered in to take a look and after some sniffing around it wandered out again and ambled off into the woods. Once the bear was gone, I raced into the cabin screaming and refused to leave it for hours. It was years before any of us kids would go out the outhouse by ourselves. Canoe Lake the way I experienced it sure left its mark on all of us.

I turn on the water tap to fill the kettle with water to make myself a cup of tea. Nothing comes out. The water pump has stopped working. I curse at it under my breath, but really I am cursing at myself. You would have thought that after coming here all these years that I'd have figured out the mechanics of its operation. But I haven't. Keeping the water system going was always the purview of my brother. I suppose it was an unconscious division of labour sort of thing. He handled the boats and the cottage infrastructure. This included the water system and the opening and closing of the cabin at the beginning and end of the season. I handled everything else in between. But this year, he's 2,000 miles away, so I'm going to have to figure it out for myself. I crawl down the steep embankment to where the pump sits in its little house by the edge of the water. It's near one of the last remaining giant white pine trees, which towers over me as I investigate. Unfortunately everything looks as it should. There are no loose fitting pipes or wires, which is most unfortunate as it means that there aren't any easy fixes. I decide that maybe it just needs priming so I crawl back up the embankment and return to the cabin and find the toolbox in the back porch.

Armed with funnel, a bailer and screwdriver I crawl back down the embankment again, undo the intake pipe and begin filling the pipe up with water. After several gallons have been added, it becomes clear that this is a problem that is beyond my ability to solve. I curse again and head back up the hill to the phone.

I call my neighbour Jim at the Thompsons' cottage. His wife Catherine's family been there since 1925. Their green and white two-story cabin was originally built by John Macklem, the owner of a Goshen, Ohio, scaffolding firm. There are no records of how he got there, only records of his attempts to sell it in the early 1920s after he'd moved his business to California and couldn't visit as frequently as he had in the past. Jim comes over and after a bit of methodical investigation and a few "Hail Mary's" thrown in for good measure, he finds a hole in the intake pipe. It's hidden beneath the brick that keeps the intake pipe resting on the bottom of the lake. I know that I would never have found that hole in a thousand years. Once again an easy solution was found for one with experience and the right tools. I'm humiliated once more. Later in the day I bring Jim a bottle of fine 12-year-old scotch to thank him for his willingness to come to my aid. It begins to storm, so Catherine suggests that I stay for dinner. Over chicken and rice she tells me her family story.

Harvey Loyst, Charles Loyst and Cousin Donald Thompson Crossing
Canor Lake, circa 1930s—Brackley Collection

Amy Faragher Loyst and
Tess Faragher Thompson

Amy with Children (left to right) Robert, Harvey and Charles—Brackley Collection

Tess on Her Honeymoon at Canoe Lake, 1927—
Brackley Collection

Amy Faragher Loyst and Tess Faragher Thompson

Cal and Amy Loyst first became acquainted with Algonquin Park by visiting their good friends, Jim and Eunice Noble. In 1920 Jim Noble was a railway conductor. He lived in Parry Sound and helped dig out the Sim's Pit railway station (later called Taylor Statten Station). He loved Algonquin Park and leased a site halfway between Wabeek Pointe and the Tom Thomson Cairn. He used to arrive by train at Canoe Lake Station and would row over to his cabin from Mowat in a flat-bottomed punt that he had. Jim was very popular on the lake and in the 1930s was anointed the first "Mayor of Canoe Lake," a designation first bestowed on Shannon Fraser some 20 years earlier.[110] Cal and Amy were among many friends and visitors that the Nobles entertained, and like so many before them, they fell in love with Algonquin Park. Each summer, they would camp with the Nobles.

In 1926 the Loysts decided to get a lease themselves and took a site to the east of the Hayhursts. Every few weeks Cal would arrive by train for a few days, laden with boxes of fresh groceries to supplement the hard goods supplied by Eaton's. As for so many others, "Eaton's Camp and Cottage Catalog" provided all of the food staples. In the 1930s and '40s, Eaton's used to offer residents at summer cottages their very own mail-order book that included just about every item one could possibly need for a cottage.[111] Everything you ordered was packed and delivered from Toronto for free to the nearest steamship dock or railway station. It was common practice in those days to order and have delivered all of the staples needed for the summer season. For the kids there was a "sunny day" box that had shovels and toys, and a "rainy day" box that included crayons and books. One time Cal and Jim decided to come up together on the train and started their vacation celebration rather early with a little imbibing. At Canoe Lake Station the conductor had to push them off the train. They slid down the luggage chute, luckily right into a boat that was waiting below.

Amy Loyst was a very avant-garde feminist and according to legend did everything better than her husband. She was a superb organizer, especially in the bush, and as a competitive breaststroke swimmer in Toronto won

---

[110]Fraser was actually anointed the Mayor of Mowat, but by 1930 Mowat had disappeared so the Mayor of Canoe Lake became the new name.

[111]An excellent article on this can be found in Cottage Life Magazine, June 2000, pg 86.

lots of trophies. Her sister Tess Faragher, who later married Cam Thompson, was a competitive diver. The sisters would skinny dip together and sun bathe nude all of the time, which was considered very risqué in those days. One story had Tess visiting her doctor in 1939, who, when commenting about the marks across her belly, was shocked speechless when Tess told him that she had fallen asleep nude in the sun and that the lines were the outline of her book. Tess was one of the first Girl Guides in Canada and through them learned about camping including setting fires, lighting lanterns and cooking outside.

Tess and Cam first came to visit the Loysts on Canoe Lake on their honeymoon in 1927. From then on they vacationed with Amy and Cal at Canoe Lake every year. Though Cam had never attended Camp Ahmek, he was a grand nephew of Ernest Thompson Seton who had visited in the summer of 1922 to teach the techniques and methods of his Woodcraft League of America. Cam's uncle Stuart Thompson (also related to Seton) was a core member of the Ahmek naturalist staff in it's early years. In 1935, the Thompson's heard that John Macklem was trying to sell his fishing camp built around 1916 near Gilmour Island and jumped at the chance to have a summer hideaway on Canoe Lake. For the first few years the Thompsons came in by train from Toronto with their three children as soon as school was out in June. Later, once Highway 60 was built, they came in by car, which would take five to six hours. Everett Farley would pick them up at the Portage Store. The family loved to go to musicals and campfires at Camp Ahmek to which all Canoe Lake residents were always invited. Amy Loyst died unexpectedly in 1942 and her sister-in-law Catherine gave up a budding career in New York to come to Canada to help Cal raise his three sons.

In the early 1940s, the cost of a typical Canoe Lake weekend was about $90, including $80 for food, $6 for gas and $2.50 for liquor. Tess kept a family log in which she recorded all of the major events that occurred around her over a 40-year period. Some typical cottage expenses included:

Cottage Expenses 1935-1975
1935 - Cottage $300 and canoe bought from camp $60
1937 - Porch built
1938 - Bought new boat $80
1939 - Stove $45

1940 - Dock $60, back porch $30, first motor $49.80

1645 - Linoleum and rugs $9.75, picnic benches $1.95

1947 - Glassed in front porch $100, porch linoleum $9.75

1948 - Kitchen cupboards $105

1951 - Lumber for dock $58, Felix Lucasavitch for labour $50

1953 - Partitions $56 (Frank built)

1954 - New boat $200, hydro installed

1955 - New 12 hp motor $200

1959 - Electric water pump $60

1960 - New cabin (for parents) $1,000

1965 - Boat repairs -$116, stove $64, straight back chairs $10

1966 - Tiled floor in living room

1969 - Added new kitchen, bathroom, hot water and showers

1971 - New shingles

1975 - Repairs to the dock $300

Tess loved to fish and, according to the family log, 1946 was a great fishing year. She set the family record by catching a 14-pound lake trout. It measured 17 inches around the belly. Her fishing style though was unique. It involved sitting on shore with her line out until some hapless fish should happen upon her hook. Where upon she would stand up, pick up the rod and march up the hill with it, the line dragging behind, until the fish hit shore. The Stringer brothers thought she was nuts. That was no way to catch a fish and they were astonished at her success.

She was also very influential with Ontario Hydro for in 1953 the Thompsons were the first leaseholders on the lake to get hydro. Some thought it was just because the first main power line went directly to Camp Wapomeo right next door. However, the truth was a bit subtler than that. Tess just happened to be making pies on the day that the installation was taking place. She took a pie, fresh from the oven over to the boys who were cutting the line. Then she suggested that there were,

> "More where this one had come from that would be just
> about ready in a hour that had their names on them if and
> when they should feel like running the hydro line over to
> her cottage." [112]

---

[112] Thompson Family Cottage Log, 1953.

In a heartbeat it was done with the cost being $10 for a pole and about a half a dozen blueberry pies. Cam Thompson died in 1980, followed in 1984 by Tess. Both came up to Canoe Lake every year until the end.[113]

Tess Thompson as a Young Girl at Swimming Championships, circa early 1920s—Brackley Collection

---

[113] In 1976, the Thompson lease was transferred to the Thompson children.

Amy Loyst with Harvey—Brackley Collection

Picnic with Hayhursts at Tea Lake (left to right) Thomas Hayhurst,
Tess Thompson, Mary Hayhurst, Jean Hayhurst—Brackley Collection

First Exotic Boat on Canoe Lake, The Ellen Vannin,
Built by Tess' Father—Brackley Collection

First Leaseholder Boat Engine
Owned by Loyst Family—Brackley Collection

143

Gillender and Krantz

Photo of Gillender and Krantz Cabin—APMA #7107 MNR Lease Archives

Gillender and Krantz

In 1923, two lively friends who were both schoolteachers arrived from the United States for a vacation at Nominigan Lodge on Smoke Lake along with a Mrs. Blanche Motley. Annie Krantz was from Philadelphia and Hannah Gillender was from England. Their intent was to start a camp for girls on Smoke Lake. They had a wonderful visit, selected some choice land on a picturesque point and in December of that year wrote a note requesting a lease to the Department.

> "Miss Gillender, being British, has been urged by many Canadians, to establish a camp catering to the Canadian girls. All being in education work, we believe we can establish an institution which will be in harmony with the spirit that decided to set aside Algonquin Park as a national playground."[114]

They unfortunately were unaware of the Department policy at the time of issuing only one lease per person and had applied for nine lease sites on Smoke Lake in their names. Why they didn't request a "license of occupation" as was the custom for activities of a commercial nature is not known. For some reason, the Department viewed this application as a "scheme to avoid paying the $75 commercial lease fee" and was not supportive of their efforts.[115] For many months the ladies corresponded with the Department trying to get their application in a form that would gain approval. Eventually, in the spring of 1924 a "license of occupation" was approved for a five-acre parcel, but by then their vision of a girls' camp faded and the ladies lost interest in the Smoke Lake property. One speculates that Taylor Statten's friendship with the Park superintendent may have brought to Taylor's attention the plans of Gillender and Krantz as soon after their arrival on the scene the Stattens decided to start Camp Wapomeo for Girls on Little Wapomeo Island. Upon visiting Canoe Lake they stumbled upon a two-story log cabin that was owned by Maude Macklem Perkins. Her brother John Macklem had built it for her in 1920 on the top of a small ridge opposite the north end of Big Wapomeo Island. The cabin had one room upstairs, one room down and a summer kitchen at the rear.

---

[114] Correspondence in the Ministry lease archives.
[115] Correspondence in the Ministry lease archives.

Alas, Mrs. Perkins had never visited Canoe Lake so the cabin had never been used. She agreed to sell it to Gillender and Krantz in 1925, who immediately settled in. Both were in love with Algonquin Park and continued to come to Canoe Lake each summer.

In the early years Gillender and Krantz had only a rowboat and were often seen rowing about the lake. It is likely that they would have been met at the train and transported to their cabin by someone on the lake. In later years they had a small wooden boat with a little 1931 vintage engine. It usually had enough juice to get them started in the morning, but not to get them back in the afternoons after their tours around the lake. In the 1940s they would hail anyone passing by and ask if they would tow them back to their dock. Customary was an invitation to afternoon tea. After they had retired to Florida, train service was no longer provided, so they would arrive in an old Buick with balding tires that looked like it barely made the trip.

One summer resident, Bob Clappison, tells a marvelous story of meeting them one year in the spring when they had just arrived at the leaseholders' dock. Bob was all of 16-years old and they asked him to help them unpack their car and load all of their summer supply of goods into their boat. Of course, being a friendly neighbour he agreed. Once the boat was loaded, they asked if he could drive them up the lake to their cabin as they were unsure of the reliability of their motor. Again Bob agreed to help them out. Once he had gotten them safely to their dock, they asked if he could help them unload all of their supplies and haul them all the way up the hill to their cabin. Once more he graciously agreed likely expecting a monetary reward for his efforts. He was eventually disappointed as his reward for all of that effort was hearty thanks and a large, fresh Florida orange.

Though they loved their spot, Gillender and Krantz echoed Louisa Blecher's concerns about the handling of garbage at the Camp Wapomeo dump that was directly west of their cabin. As they wrote so poignantly in 1926,

> "Not only is the smell of garbage and disinfectant distressing but the fact that wash water is going straight into the lake is a menace to our health."[116]

---

[116] Correspondence in the Ministry lease archives.

Another problem with the dump was that it attracted bears, a major nuisance for them and later their neighbours, the Adaskins. As the nearest cabin worth visiting, bears were constantly breaking in and frightening the two half to death. As Annie wrote to the Park superintendent:

> "Our departure was hastened last fall because of a large black bear, which broke into the kitchen and spent a whole night upsetting things and us. We restored the place to perfect order but on arriving this year found it again in complete disorder. Just this week we had two visits from a big bear and are afraid."[117]

Another big concern for them in the 1930s was the number of break-ins and robberies taking place up and down the shoreline from Canoe Lake Station to their lease site. It is unclear why, but their cottage was broken into nine times in 13 years or so they wrote in 1936. The culprits were never found until November 1936 when two men from Haliburton were arrested. They had been operating a housebreaking and theft ring in the Park. Though most of the goods stolen were believed to have been disposed of through second-hand stores in Toronto, the Department was able to recover a few things. A list was forwarded to many Canoe Lake residents to see if any of the property found belonged to them. It is unclear how leaseholders might have identified their property since so many of the items were things that most cottagers might have had in their possession.

In their later years, Frances and Murray Adaskin who settled just around the point from them to the west and were their designated saviours. Gillender and Krantz had an old school bell that they would ring when they needed help. When it rang, one of the Adaskins would hot-foot it over there to see what was up.[118] Francis Adaskin was a singer under contract with Canadian National Railway and sang at all of their hotels across Canada. Her husband Murray was a composer and professor of music. In 1946 they had spent the summer renting the cabin at Wabeek Pointe and wanted a site of their own. The next summer they took out a lease on the entryway to Whiskey Jack Creek. Everett Farley built a main cabin for them and a studio where they kept their piano. There are several stories as

---

[117]Correspondence in the Ministry lease archives. A couple of years later, four bears had to be shot in the vicinity.
[118]Today that school bell hangs in the Adaskin/Nelson cottage.

to how the piano got there. The most entertaining tells of when the Camp Ahmek barge was called into service. It transported the piano across Canoe Lake from Canoe Lake Station. Another story recounted that the piano was brought down the creek to the cottage floating on a raft of canoes. A note from Dr. Charles Hendry, (Chick) one of the first counselors at Camp Ahmek remembers well that day.

> "There was no road, so they fastened six canoes together and ferried it to the camp site on Canoe Lake. Scott Malcolm, who played concert piano, and Reginald Golden mounted the shaky raft and began to play and sing 'Danny Boy' as they paddled down the lake."[119]

Each summer, after they had settled in residence, "The Chief" would invite Murray and Frances to Ahmek and Wapomeo to play or visit with musically inclined campers. Folks at the north end used to be serenaded frequently by Frances when she practiced her scales and performances from the end of their dock. Murray later composed the "Algonquin Symphony," a very famous piece of music at least to Taylor Statten Camps alumni, and also the music for the Camp Ahmek evening grace. In the mid-'50s, Hannah died and by 1959 so did Annie and except for a few stories, they disappeared from Canoe Lake community consciousness. In 1961 Annie's son, Frank Krantz, tried to assume the lease. There was such confusion as to the rules for inheriting a "joint tenant lease" that it took until 1967 to sort out the lease title. In 1974, he sold his lease back to the crown and the beautiful Macklem cabin was removed the following year. All that remains up on the hill today of that beautiful cabin is the remains of the huge fireplace and some rusted pieces of tin.

---

[119] The Toronto Star, November 1972.

Nov. 12th.,1936

Miss H. F. Gillender,
c/o C.C.Mellor Memorial Library,
Edgewood, Pittsburgh, Pa.

Dear Madam;-

　　　　　　With the arrest by rangers of two men from
Haliburton, it is believed that the matter of housebreaking
and thefts at Canoe Lake during the past few years has been
cleared up. The following articles are being held at Algonquin Park, pending identification and claim. Other articles
which were stolen and are not listed are believed to have
been disposed of through second-hand stores in Toronto.

Stolen goods, recovered, and held at Algonquin Park -

1 pr. red blankets	1 blow torch
1 purple and orange sweater	1 pair binoculars
1 hunting knife	1 hot water bottle
1 piece of chain	1 brown tent
1 silk tent	5 rubber sheets
1 brass Aladdin lamp	3 canoes
1 pr. khaki breeches	3 paddles
1 can opener	1 fishing rod
1 thermometer	1 metal tackle box
1 nature book "Birds"	2 fishing reels
1 Delta Apollo hand lantern	2 packsacks
2 pickle silver dessert spoons	1 dunnage bag
1 pkg. Coleman mantles and pick	1 pr. grass shears
1 pr. red Hudson Bay blankets	~~1 fishing rod~~
1 rim for holding lamp shade	Assorted baits, hooks
1 cushion with brown leather cover.	and lures

　　　　　　We would appreciate hearing from you if you can
positively identify any of the above articles.

　　　　　　　　　　Yours very truly,

fam/jsw　　　　　　　　　Superintendent.

The Summer Widows

Joe Runner and Kids Head to the Camp Ahmek Circus, circa mid-1960s.
Author in bow—Clemson Collection

The Summer Widows

In the late 1940s and early '50s, a number of alumni from Camp Wapomeo and Camp Ahmek decided to settle on Canoe Lake, mostly at the south end. Though there were by now a number of different social groups on the lake, for those with kids there was constant visiting back and forth. If wind and the weather was cooperative, each day's outdoor activities would include swimming, water skiing, sailing, canoeing, hiking to various landmarks or picnicking anywhere there was an open rock or clearing. On rainy days there would be a slew of card or board games to play. Most families had speedboats for the adults and small 1- or 2-horsepower "putt-putts" that the kids would use. Once you were 10 years old or so these small boats were the ticket to lakeside independence. It meant that you could drive yourself over and back to a friend's cabin and explore the mysteries of the lake without parental supervision. One downside was that the kids would constantly leave their belongings at each other's cabins. One year there were so many items found at one cottage at the end of the summer that the mother hung them all from a huge T-shaped piece of wood mounted against the boathouse. Everyone who went by could see it and in this way all of the belongings were returned to their rightful owners in no time flat.

The highlights of the social season for the adults were the mid-summer costume ball and the annual end-of-summer corn roast. The shoal at the south end was also a frequent weekend party spot. On sunny, calm days, a raft would be anchored there and the party would go on until the food and drinks ran out. One summer two hearty souls spent an entire day out on the shoal playing poker at a card table set up in the shallow water, while sitting on beach chairs under an umbrella. A number of other memorable parties of those years involved Joe Runner. Joe Runner was an actor, a playwright, a director and an artist who lived in New York City. During the mid-1950s, he was the Ahmek Theatre director and produced a number of memorable productions of "Oklahoma" and other musicals. He loved kids and one year he convinced all of the kids on the lake to dress up as various Peter Pan characters. He took them all up to participate in the annual Circus Day at Camp Ahmek. Joe used to write about Tom Thomson and loved to impersonate him, so the first memorable Joe Runner party was one held to celebrate the anniversary of Tom Thomson's death. The party was well under way when suddenly there was the unmistakable sound of heavy chains clanking. Rushing down to the dock to see what was up, the guests could hear moans and more clanking. Suddenly up out of the water came Joe Runner as the ghost of Tom Thomson. He was covered with slime and ketchup with a flashlight shining on his face that made him look like an apparition from the dead.

Another time he organized a celebration at the lumber mill ruins up on Potter Creek. A bar was set up next to the remains of the concrete wall and decorated with driftwood. For some strange and unknown reason one guest brought a little cannon and started shooting a cannon ball through a hole in the wall. After the first one blasted there was dead silence for 15 seconds, then the driftwood centerpiece fell to the floor and everyone screamed, convinced that the ruins were about to fall on their heads. Then it started to rain cats and dogs. A guest went out and got a tarp. Everyone grappled with a section and propped it up with paddles over their heads to keep out the rain. As the tarp got full of water, people started to push out the water over the edges of the tarp with the ends of their paddles. The end result was not pretty. Without warning the tarpaulin ripped apart and an entire wall of water fell onto everyone's head.

A third Joe Runner escapade was at one of the annual costume parties. Two leaseholders were paddling over to the party when they heard a motorboat start up from down the lake. At full speed they could hear it heading their way, and suddenly there was total silence. As they rounded Popcorn Island and were heading towards the dock, they heard slosh, slosh, slosh sounds. Curious as to what it was, they turned on their flashlights just in time to see a lady in a lovely white dress and broad-rimmed hat walking on the water. It was Joe Runner in his party costume. He'd forgotten that the water level was too shallow on the east side of Popcorn Island and he'd run Gibby's boat straight into the rocks and was now trying to make it to shore. The water in his hiking boots was making the sloshing sound as he moved from rock to rock. But it didn't end there. Gibby's boat had a huge hole in the bow. Later in the evening the men gathered round for an extensive discussion as to the best way to pull it out of the water before it sank to the bottom.[120]

In 1953, a decision was made that the lake needed to have a yacht club and so the South Shore Yacht and Country Club was born. Its inaugural

---

[120] Joe Runner accidentally drowned in 1993 while trying to swim across Potter Creek.

meeting was held on Sunday April 5, 1953. The club's objective was to be a non-profit organization devoted to cultural activities on Canoe Lake. The Chief and Wam Stringer were appointed as the Honorary Commodores. In typical chauvinistic fashion of the time, at the first meeting a rather lengthy discussion ensued as to the voting status of wives and girl-friends, who were referred to in those days as "baby dolls." A "baby doll" was defined as any female over 16 years of age who could carry two pails of water or would do what she was told over a visiting weekend. It was agreed eventually that all wives would have an equal vote; daughters and sons over 20 years of age and "baby dolls" were granted half a vote. Husbands were advised that they could control the votes of their wives, if the wife was absent. Membership fees were set at $9 to be initiated and $5 per year per family. Though meetings were only held during the first few years of the club's existence, it did establish several lake customs that have lived on ever since:

- Yearly sweepstakes to guess the ice break-up date. Today it is called the annual "Ice Out" and votes are cast via the Internet.
- An annual sailing regatta that still occurs every August.
- An annual "Commodore's Cocktail Party" that for the past four years has taken the form of a canoeing and swimming regatta followed by a community barbecue.

The last formal meeting of the club occurred in the fall of 1954. No serious motions were proffered since it was apparent that members had some difficulty recognizing each other due to the wearing of city clothes, not old flannel shirts and gas-stained work pants.

Every woman on the lake knew or learned quickly how to paddle a canoe, handle a motorboat and successfully go on canoe trips. One time a leaseholder got himself in big trouble by arguing with his future wife while they were out for an evening paddle. His fiancée stopped the canoe by a stump and told him to get out. He foolishly complied and she paddled off. It took some time and a lot of yelling before a neighbour rescued him. Canoes were usually easy to manage except in high winds, but boats were another story. One mistake and your boat or motor would be at the bottom of the lake. My mother's experience provided a good example.

One of the neigbours across the lake had sold to my father a used Z-77 racing boat, with a souped-up 35-horsepower Evinrude engine. This boat could fly across the water, so my father named it "The Queen of the Seas." He would spend endless hours repairing and repainting her hull its distinctive red, white and blue colours. One year my mother Isabel was up at the cottage alone dealing with three kids who had just come down with the flu. In her rush to get everyone inside after visiting some neighbours up the lake and the excitement of racing across the lake in advance of a huge rainstorm, she had accidentally left the boat tied with the stern facing north. That night huge waves broke over the stern until the painter broke. Down went the boat to the bottom of the lake. When Isabel came down to the dock to bail out the boats the next morning, all that was visible above the water line was the tip of the bow. Needless to say panic set in. She called Wam and Jimmy Stringer who marshaled up the few men available on a weekday. After much discussion, the group attached a winch to the bow, and slowly raised the boat from the depths of the lake bailing furiously so that it's keel wouldn't snap. The engine was immediately taken to a neighbours dock and taken apart piece by piece and left to dry in the sunshine. That afternoon Jimmy Stringer put it all back together again and pulled the cord. Surprise of all surprises, it started immediately and the day was saved. Several bottles of good scotch were the reward for the saviors. In the mid-'70s, the boathouse roof collapsed one winter and crushed the Queen in such a way that it wasn't repairable. That souped-up engine still sits under the Clemson cabin and in 1997 was taken out to see if it still worked. To everyone's surprise after a little fiddling it started right up again as good as new.

There were conflicting views on the lake amongst the women about the "fun" of canoe trips. Some of them had been campers at Camp Wapomeo and loved it and would often accompany their husbands, fiancées and their buddies on these excursions. For others, canoe trips were what one endured in order to talk about afterwards. Once Wam Stringer, who was often working in those days as a fishing guide, took a group on a fishing trip to Green Lake (now known as Happy Isle). He started breakfast by making and flipping pancakes using a method that one wife thought left much to be desired. Wam got in a huff so she took over and as she flipped her first batch of pancakes, one landed on Wam's head. Needless to say, for the rest of the trip, flipping pancakes became Wam's job. Another classic story of these early days involved a pair of leaseholder newlyweds who went on a canoe trip for their honeymoon. Both were experienced trippers. They arrived back to their cabin wet and tired after a long and arduous trip, only to find that unnamed fellow leaseholders had taken every piece of their furniture from the cabin and packed it into their small sleeping bunkee. They were not impressed, but fellow leaseholders found it to be tremendously amusing.

For others without camping experience, canoe trips were a nightmare. Another of my mother Isabel's experiences were of this sort. My father Stan was not known for his planning abilities, and so with 24 hours notice, Isabel packed up the needed equipment and supplies for our first grand canoe tripping experiment. We nearly never made it past the first portage from Canoe Lake to Smoke Lake. With three kids and two adults, the idea was we could go far because we would need to cross each portage only twice. Father would carry one canoe overhead and mother and daughter would hand-carry the other. The two boys would carry all of the paddles and life jackets and small day packs. Father and mother would recross the portage and bring the packs. Unfortunately, no one had any idea of the strength needed in the arms nor how awkward it was to hand carry an aluminum canoe upright. A few yards down the trail, both of the women collapsed in a heap ready and anxious to call the whole thing off and return to the safety of the cottage. After a good collective cry, further encouragement from Stan and acknowledgement that all portages would need to be crossed several times, they continued on their way. The weather stayed clear and calm, so though slow, the trip ended up being a glorious experience for all involved. For all of us kids, these trips were a marvelous time. In hindsight, it's not clear that it was as much fun for my mother. The last major trip was after all of the kids had many years' tripping experience at Camp Ahmek and Camp Wapomeo. That time portages were traversed once, campsites set up in a heartbeat and meals whipped up that during the five days were a culinary delight. What a difference a little experience made!

One constant in all of our lives then, and still today, was the huge numbers of visitors who would rent canoes from the Portage Store and spend their day on Canoe Lake. Often colloquially called "rinky dinks" or "rinks," these visitors often had little or no skill in canoeing and were easily recognized in their Portage Store or Algonquin Outfitter labeled aluminum and later fiberglass canoes. Their inability to steer properly meant that they had a tendency to zigzag across the lake as they tried to go from one spot to another. They had a severe propensity for overloading canoes either with people or belongings, and a total lack of awareness as to the appropriate way to sit in a canoe, i.e., knees below the gunwale to lower the center of gravity. Few had knowledge of the "J-stroke," bow draws or any other of the basics of canoemanship. The Ministry of Natural Resources had given up on trying to police their activity in any major way, except for the occasional lake visit by the Ontario Provincial Police to enforce the boating regulations. The Portage Store staff tried to provide some of the basic instruction in canoeing, so as to reduce the most blatant errors in judgement, but it was an uphill battle.

This meant that the leaseholders had assumed custodial responsibility for keeping an eye out for the antics of these day visitors. It became an integral part of everyday life on Canoe Lake. Every week there would be a number of rescues of dumped canoes or counseling when people were in danger of getting hurt. At times it seemed like common sense had been left behind in the cities or at the Park gates. Many naïve visitors would head out of Portage Store Bay in a strong north headwind and not realize how tired they would get when not paddling properly. Canoeists were constantly being blown onto Windy Isle or onto leaseholders docks. Others wouldn't know how to read the map, or didn't purchase one and would end up paddling around Whiskey Jack Creek, Ahmek Bay or Ghost Walk Creek, trying to find the entryway to Joe Lake. Still others would stay out on the lake during a thunderstorm not realizing the danger of being hit by lightning.

All of the wives were well acquainted with basics of water canoe rescue techniques. In calm weather most visitors could eventually make their way up or down the lake given enough time. But when there was a strong north or west wind, or foul weather set in, disaster would strike. It's frightening to think of the number of wallets, cameras, car and house keys and even diving equipment that now rests on the bottom of Canoe Lake. Once a fellow dumped just off a dock on the west shore with what looked like thousands of dollars of camera equipment that wasn't strapped into the canoe. Another time a honeymooning couple decided to change places in the canoe in the middle of the lake. They dumped and lost everything. One time two leaseholders, coming out of Portage Bay, came across a sinking fold-up boat. Inside was a man and two small kids without life jackets. They rescued the kids but made the man paddle the waterlogged boat back to the dock by himself. Another time two canoeists approached the Adaskins' property at dusk asking if it was a campsite. It became apparent that they spoke limited English, had no car to return to, not much food and little camping skill. The Adaskins escorted them to an abandoned lease site with instructions to move on at daylight. Investigation the next day revealed that the group had set a fire on top an old pine root, which was still smoldering, and had left garbage strewn about. The Adaskins put out the fire and tidied up the site. But the most terrifying was the year one leaseholder found a couple paddling around the lake with their 6-month-old baby, life jacketless, strapped into a car seat, which in turn had been tied to the center thwart of the canoe.

One year an attempt was made to rescue a German couple who had dumped their canoe in Portage Bay. With great difficulty the rescuer was able to get the woman into his boat, but was totally unsuccessful with the husband. The only solution was to tow him to the Portage Store beach, so that he could walk out of the water himself. An even funnier story was the time a French couple stopped in at a leaseholder's dock to ask for directions. All they had with them for several days in the woods was a baguette, a round of salami and a bottle of wine. They were expecting to find boulangeries and hostels along the route, as was traditional in the south of France.

Motherly concern about the activities of naïve canoeists reflected not just a slight sense of superiority as a result of their better canoeing, tripping and boating skills, but real concerns about visitor safety. Over the years there were several accidental deaths on the lake, including one visitor who dumped and drowned on the east shore one late October day, and another who drowned one summer just off the Portage Store docks. Though not wilderness anymore in the purest sense of the word, experiences on the lake had taught all leaseholders to be respectful of the danger lurking all around. Dumping a canoe into cold water was no joke, especially in early spring or fall or in inclement weather. Getting lost on a trail, being attacked by bears or other wild animals by leaving food in inappropriate places (like inside a tent) and accidents with axes or fire were frequent occurrences. Though today wilderness rescue is much easier than it was in previous decades, Huntsville hospital was still over 50 kilometers away so the potential danger in the forest could not be minimized. Knowing that help was, at a minimum, hours away and if in the interior, days away, made for cautious leaseholders.

Even today it continues to be frightening to watch those who naively walk into dangerous situations without any idea of potential risks. All leaseholders take on the responsibility willingly of keeping an eye for the visitors around them and the safety of each other. Every few years the Canoe Lake and District Leaseholders Association would express concern to the Portage Store and to the Ministry about these challenges that usually went unanswered. The Ministry had decided that experience was the best of teachers and didn't want to get into the position of being babysitters for the public.

On canoe trips, visitors were known to bring just about everything but the kitchen sink including row boats, lawn chairs, hard-backed suitcases and tons of beer. You name it, someone would bring it on a canoe trip. They would sit on their haunches and stare when Camp Wapomeo trippers would pull up to a portage with their skilled landings and departures. The person in the bow would jump out as soon as they reached the shore and sit on the bow to steady the canoe. The person in the center would toss out the packs and hop out. Both would then pick up their packs grab the lifejackets and paddles and head off down the trail. The person in the stern would pull the canoe up out of the water, easily toss it onto her shoulders and off she'd go down the portage. All of this would take place in only a few minutes.

The best story of the effect of this on exhausted novice canoe trippers was from two longstanding leaseholders that had decided to take a fishing trip to Red Pine Bay in the late '50s. They made camp at Hogan Lake and then crossed to Lake LaMuir to fish. Before they left, a pilot friend who flew a Beaver aircraft had agreed to drop in and pick up their gear on their last day. This he did and left them with the canoe, fishing rods, a small motor attached to the canoe and an empty brown bottle of Ballantine scotch that held their drinking water. At the Burnt Island portage, one was carrying the canoe and the other was carrying the pack and the motor. They met some visitors (complete with coolers, lawn chairs and suitcases) who had been out on trip for two days. They were going back for the rest of their mountain of gear and were shocked to see the two with nothing but their canoe and fishing tackle. After inquiring, they were told that when tripping a tent wasn't needed because sleeping under the canoe was preferred. Food didn't need to be hauled in as there were plenty of blueberries to pick and fish to be caught. After the lecture, each took a swig at the supposed bottle of scotch, wiped their mouths off with the back of their hands and paddled off down the lake. They could hear the visitors mumbling to each other, "That's how we need to do it next year!!!"

On Canoe Lake itself, most leaseholders had to deal from time to time with unwanted visits from those who thought that cottage docks were great picnicking spots built for their convenience and use. Often left behind would be a collection of empty beer and wine bottles. One year a leaseholder arrived to find a group using his shower. Another time two women decided to stop and go topless sun-bathing on the beach by the Camp Ahmek baseball diamond. They didn't notice that their prime sunning spot was in the middle of a boys' camp. Every year there was at least one group that decided that Wabeek Pointe was a perfect camping spot. It got so bad on Popcorn Island (as it was often the first stopping point on the way up the lake) that it became known by many of the local kids as Pee Pot Island. The same problem would happen at the Tom Thomson Totem Pole and Cairn. Visitors would often wander down to Hayhursts thinking that their outhouse was a public facility. For those who lived on the east shore it was a different problem. Day visitors would hike up the path that ran behind the cottages from the leaseholder dock to Lighthouse Point. They would go on down to the water and enjoy themselves sunning and swimming off of leaseholder docks. These leaseholders also bore the brunt of the canoe rescue work.

Many mothers enjoyed weekdays with the children, with husbands working Monday through Friday jobs in their hometowns until visiting for the weekend. The women had plenty of social life and excitement, with children's activities and a good share of canoe rescues, but they faced plenty of challenges, too. One of the big ones was the constant presence of bears. In those days environmental issues were not the concern that they are today. Each lease had its own private garbage dump within reasonable walking distance of the cabin. It didn't take long for the bears to figure out that fishing food out of garbage dumps was much easier than picking berries or eating bugs out of an overturned log. In poor berry crop years, the bears would be out in full force, which was quite terrifying even for those familiar with them. One resident, tells the story of hearing noises on the roof every morning. She figured it was just raccoons or squirrels and didn't think much of it. But one morning she decided to investigate and found a young bear sitting up on the roof close to the stovepipe. The heat from the fireplace made it nice and warm and the view of the sunrise over the lake was spectacular. Smart bear!

Another story involved a woman at the north end who was an excellent hostess and would hold marvelous dinner parties. One year, a bear smelled a cooking roast and crawled in through the kitchen window to help himself. The hostess saw him and came storming into the kitchen cabin waving her broom yelling "Shoo, Shoo!" She was only five feet tall and 100 pounds soaking wet, so to see her go after this massive bear must have been quite a sight. What a feisty woman!!!

In the 1960s bear problems got worse as it was suggested that burning garbage rather than just dumping it was more environmentally correct. This idea turned out to be a disaster. The smell of burning steak or chicken bones would attract the bears from miles around. One great bear experience happened at the Adaskins'. They used to burn their garbage in an old stone incinerator out the back of their cabin. One year Frances came out onto the back porch and saw this huge bear's rear end. It had wandered over from the old Whiskey Jack garbage site and was nosing around the incinerator. She ran inside and grabbed a pot and ran outside, banging it wildly to scare away the bear. The bear got so frightened that it totally smashed up the stone incinerator. Many years later, her niece came out on the deck after hearing a red squirrel going crazy. She nearly ran into a bear that was out there observing her husband who was sitting on the dock reading a book. The bear took off into the bush and few minutes later he reappeared about 200 yards down the shore. It then jumped in the water and swam across the entrance to Whiskey Jack Creek. Not only could this bear swim very fast, but was surprisingly buoyant, so it looked like a huge black raft was racing across the channel.

Another classic bear story was Isobel Cowie and Marg McColl's experience during one of their early visits to the Park in the 1940s. They had spent their two-week holiday with Frank Braucht. Near the end, Frank decided that Isobel need a further rest cure in the Park. He had other guests coming so he set up a tent on the ridge nearby for Marg and Isobel. They all went into Huntsville for provisions and put them in huge cans that were guaranteed to be bear proof. Down to the lake the girls went for their afternoon swim. A little while later they headed back up the ridge. Marg was carrying two buckets of water on a yoke swung over her shoulders. Suddenly Isobel let out a yell and grabbed an axe and ran up the trail at full speed in her bare feet. A huge black bear was at their food and was just finishing the last of their bread including the wrapper. That ended the rest cure. They successfully scrounged dinner from Frank's other visitors that night but were unable to drive the image of that bear from the embers of the campfire. That night Marg slept with her head at the tent door and was awakened in the night by a loud snuffling in her ear. She sat up screaming, "Get out! Get out!" The next morning they thanked Frank kindly but left quickly for home.

The best bear story on the lake however, involved Islay McFarlane. One summer day after Frank Braucht's death, Islay had gone to get groceries at the Portage Store. When she got back she got out of the boat and went inside the cabin to find on the dining room floor a dumped sugar bowl, and a cookie jar in pieces. She slowly approached the kitchen area in time to see a huge black bear storm out the back door. On closer inspection Islay discovered that it had gotten into the fridge and attacked the fat jar, spilling grease over everything. In a panic, Islay phoned Jimmy Stringer to ask if he had a gun. She was afraid that the bear would come back and wanted to be ready if it did. Jimmy allegedly called the Park Headquarters and got permission from the Ministry to shoot the bear if it did return. He headed over to McFarlanes'. Sure enough, a little while later the bear did come back. As soon as he saw it, Jimmy picked up the gun and chased it down the path yelling, "Fresh meat! Fresh meat!" He came back awhile later saying that he had shot it and buried it out back in the woods. A tall tale perhaps, as it is hard to imagine the diminutive Jimmy being able to dig a hole in ground full of rocks and roots big enough to bury a huge black bear. Nevertheless, Islay rewarded him with dinner and a strong drink.

Chapter 6
The Ghosts

Mary Percival

The Ghosts

It's past midnight as I head out across the lake in my green chestnut canoe. It was one of the last made by the now defunct Peterborough Canoe Company in 1977 and has held up well after over 25 years of use. I've just had a delightful dinner with John Ridpath, the lake's master storyteller and chief laser skipper. I easily slip in behind the middle thwart facing the stern and push off from the dock. The water is as smooth as glass and the silence is complete. My paddle enters the water and I begin the hard pull of the "Ahmek Stroke." No splash is heard as the paddle curves and twists in my hand in one fluid motion. The muscles of my upper arm and shoulder barely move but provide the power to the stroke. The full moon is about to set and looks huge when compared to the dark hills just below on the horizon. Because it is late fall there are few lights from fellow cottagers to light the way, so I aim for the two giant white pine trees that can be seen on the opposite shore that managed to escape the logging axe over 100 years ago. They must have been too small at the time to remove and now survey the scene with majestic superiority. The loons have finished their evening feed, as has our local resident beaver, who usually ventures out across the bay at dusk looking for some fresh tree shoots to feast on.

As I paddle along, the Canoe Lake women that I haven't been able to find out much about come to mind. First there's Helen Dance who bought George Webb's red rolled asphalt sided cabin in 1939 and stayed every summer for over 10 years. George was another unknown early settler who built at the south end in 1923 and apparently was associated with the building of the incline railway in Hamilton. All that is known about Helen is that she was the secretary for the Canoe Lake and District Leaseholders Association for several years just before her death in 1951. Unfortunately her cabin was very close to the very popular Buffalo Point campsite. Its frequent visitors were a source of some trouble to her. As she wrote in a 1946 letter to the Department:

> *"May I point out the great need for a privy at Buffalo Point camp site on Canoe Lake. As my lot is adjacent to this there have been several occasions this summer when campers have trespassed on my property and made use of my outhouse. Not*

always leaving it in a desirable condition. They have paid no attention to a "Private" sign that I put up. As this campsite is constantly made use of, I feel that this is a matter, which should be brought to your attention."[121]

Then there is Eleanor Martin, a retired schoolteacher who in 1936 leased a site on the mainland right behind Little Wapomeo Island. Prior to that she had been living in the broken down old hospital on the hill above the old chip-yard that another family member (maybe a brother-in-law, R. Shaw) had leased from Shannon Fraser in 1916. It was a big, white house that in its later years seemed to be held up by only a single tree stump. She ordered for her new lease, a ready-made "Kakabeka" cabin that she saw in a catalog from Toronto. Today the hospital site is covered with trees, but in those days the remains of the chip yard stretched way out in front of her cabin as far as the eye could see. Miss Martin was a real Canoe Lake character. Each day she would apparently take a daily walk to the post office to collect her mail, allegedly dressed in long, black, heavy clothes with a fur stole around her neck. She used to roam by herself far into the woods to pick blueberries. Jennie Armstrong was very concerned about her and would send various members of the Armstrong clan over everyday to check on her. According to local folklore, she might have been fearful for her safety in the woods as she always brought with her a police dog whose primary job, one presumes, was to frighten off any venturesome bears or unwanted visitors.

She was also very artistic and organized a quilting club that Couchie joined. Couchie still has a quilt that Miss Martin made and gave to her at one time maybe at the time of her marriage to Dr. Harry Ebbs. She also held Bible study classes, though it is not clear who came to such meetings. They may have been just a guise for the local women to get together and socialize. One year she got herself into a bit of trouble with the Department by openly requesting that the Department advertise that she had a furnished cabin available with a double bed for $6 per week. The Department thought she was setting up a commercial enterprise which was prohibited for private leaseholders – though in some cases overlooked (such as for Edith Webb and Gertrude Baskerville). Once she had assured the Department that she had no interest in establishing a commercial venture the confusion was eventually settled to everyone's satisfaction. She died in 1946.

---

[121] Correspondence in the Ministry lease archives.

Another free spirit was Dottie Davis from Richmond, Virginia, who moved over from Camp Wapomeo to become Ahmek's first female sailing instructor in 1942. Dottie had come to Wapomeo in 1930 and in her later years was one of the few who could remember camp life when it was on Little Wap not on big Wapomeo Island. She later became a pilot for the U.S. Air Force and had a job ferrying planes in the off season. She chose a site at the south end and camped there for many years. She was unable to build a cabin due to materials shortages after WWII and in 1951 sold her lease after she moved to California. She died of breast cancer in 1994. And what became of Leila Stringer Grenke, the eldest daughter of Kate and Jack Stringer? She married Hank Grenke who became another jack-of-all-trades on Canoe Lake. In the 1940s and '50s, she ran the Algonquin Hotel for George Merrydew and lived in George Rowe's old cottage down by the water next to the former Colson Outfitting Store. She befriended and more or less adopted one set of eventual leaseholders that came to Joe Lake to go on a canoe trip for their honeymoon. Once she found out that they were newlyweds, she insisted that they spend the night at her cottage. Nine months later their son was born. From that time on Leila was convinced that he had been conceived in her bed. After the Algonquin Hotel had been sold, Merrydew died and left Leila and Hank their cabin. Unfortunately it was destroyed by fire in 1964. And what about Mrs. Ratan, the Canoe Lake train station foreman's wife, who will go down in perpetuity as the woman in 1898 who told people not to spit on the floor. I wonder who was she and how frustrated she must have become to write such a creative sign.

But the woman that I am most curious about is the elusive Winifred Trainor. Her father Hugh had come to Canoe Lake as the logging foreman for the Huntsville Lumber Company, which was logging west of Canoe Lake. He wanted a summer vacation spot, so leased "The Manse" in 1912. Hugh had two daughters, Marie, who married Roy McCormick and settled in the USA, and Winifred who worked as a bookkeeper in Huntsville. In 1932 Hugh suddenly died and the lease for "The Manse" was transferred to Winifred who wintered in her parents' house in Huntsville, but spent most of her summers at Canoe Lake. According to Amy Loyst's son Harvey, she was the "Belle of the Ball" in those days. She never married, was a loyal member of the Canoe Lake and District Leaseholders Association and died in 1963. To those who knew her she was intimidating and opinionated but for the most part very well respected and admired. She was known to keep an eye on the little grave in the Canoe Lake Cemetery where Tom Thomson had temporarily been buried. In her later life she became more eccentric, according to Roy MacGregor, "not even allowing herself the luxury of hot running water." Over the years there has always been lots of whispered tales and conflicting stories of how she was Tom Thomson's love interest. It was common knowledge in Huntsville and around the lake that he had left her some hand painted tea cups and several of his paintings and drawings which she later left to her nephew in her will. But none of these tales was ever confirmed or denied by her. Her remaining family on Canoe Lake won't reveal her secrets if she has any. I found only one relevant reference to Thomson in a note she had written to the Park superintendent in 1954. She intimated that she was meeting with Dr. Bill Little and a Colonel McCurry of the National Art Gallery in Ottawa to discuss the research that Little was doing for his book on the Tom Thomson mystery. Of apparent concern to her was an article about Thomson that had appeared that spring in MacLean's magazine. She was apparently anxious to right the many wrongs that had been written about Tom, commenting that it had been 37 years to the day since "Tom lost his life on Canoe Lake."

Suddenly it gets dark as the moon partly disappears behind a cloud and I notice that a mist has gathered around me. I look up from the water and see a motion to my left. A gray-green shadow is coming towards me. I recognize the canoeist in the stern as a fellow "master canoeist." Like mine, his paddling stroke makes no sound. He seems to be tall and lean with straight dark hair that curls slightly over his ears. His angular face looks familiar but I don't know where from. There is a young woman in the bow. Her hair is pulled back in a fashion not seen in decades and her dress, with its tight bodice and flowing skirts, is totally unsuitable for today's canoeist. I gradually become aware that it is Winifred. As if reading my thoughts, she smiles shyly and nods her head. I can see now that her companion is Tom Thomson. His trademark fishing rod hangs out of the stern and his paint pallet and case are on the bottom of the canoe at his feet. I can't tell if he's trolling or not, it is too dark and the mists swirl around him. As they pass me by he raises his paddle in the customary Canoe Lake salute. I do a reverse draw to turn my canoe around and pursue them. But the mists close in and in a heartbeat they are gone. I lay my paddle across the thwart and rest for a moment, hoping that the mists will part again and enable me see once more. But they do not. I gaze up at the sparkling stars that blanket the sky overhead and wonder if the few that seem to be sparkling brighter than the rest really are the spirits of those keeping watch over us all. I turn my canoe around again and resume my slow paddle home. The moon dips below the horizon and the resident loons start up their deep mournful cry. I wonder if my imagination was playing tricks with me or whether the mists, like at Avalon, parted for a moment and let me see.

Author, Gaye Clemson, Paddling on Canoe Lake, 2002

About the Author:

Gaye I. Clemson has spent part of just about every summer for the last 48 years on the shores of Canoe Lake in Algonquin Park. Inspired by a 1996 Canoe Lake history she became curious about the settlement stories of fellow leaseholders who had inhabited the lake since 1905. For four years she and her children explored Canoe Lake's shores and visited neighhours, collecting along the way a remarkable set of word portraits of some of Canoe Lake's finest women. This book is the second of a series that captures on paper the lives of a group of very resilient women who lived at various times on Canoe Lake. When not acting in her role as Canoe Lake Historian, the author can be found in Capitola, California, with her twin 8-year-old boys running a small technology market research and strategy consulting firm.

Bibliography

1. Addison, O. *Early Days in Algonquin Park*, McGraw-Hill, Ryerson, Toronto, 1974.
2. Bice, R. *Along the Trail with Ralph Bice in Algonquin Park*, Natural Heritage/Natural History Inc, Toronto,1980.
3. Lambert R. S. *Renewing Nature's Wealth*, Ontario Department of Lands and Forests, Toronto, 1967.
4. Little W.T., *Tom Thomson Mystery*, McGraw Hill Ryerson Ltd., Toronto, 1970.
5. Saunders, A., *The Algonquin Story*, Ontario Department of Lands and Forests, Toronto, 1946.
6. Addison, O., with Elizabeth Harwood, *Tom Thomson—The Algonquin Years*, Ryerson Press, Toronto, 1969.
7. Town, H. and Silcox, D., *Tom Thomson – Silence and the Storm*, McClelland and Stewart, Toronto, 1977.
8. Pigeon M., McCormick, 1995, *Living at Brulé Lake Algonquin Park 1936-1950*, published by the author in 1993 and by the Friends of Algonquin Park in 1995.
9. MacGregor, R., 1999, *A Life in the Bush – Lessons from My Father*, Penguin Books, Toronto, 1999.
10. Meehan, B. (curator), Millard, L. (text), *Algonquin Memories – Tom Thomson in Algonquin Park*, Exhibition for the Algonquin Gallery in Algonquin Park, 1998.
11. Garland, G.D., (compiler), *Glimpses of Algonquin Park*, Friends of Algonquin Park, Algonquin Park, 1989.
12. Wright, H.E. Mooney, *Joe Lake: Reminiscences of an Algonquin Park Ranger's Daughter*, HEW Enterprises, Eganville, 1999.
13. Tozer, R., and Strickland, D., *A Pictorial History of Algonquin Park*, Ministry of Natural Resources, 1980.
14. Lundell, L. (editor), Lloyd, D. - (concept), *Fires of Friendship: Eighty Years of the Taylor Statten Camps*, Fires of Friendship Books, Toronto, 2000.

15. Shaw, B., *Canoe Lake Algonquin Park – Tom Thomson and Other Mysteries*, General Store Publishing House, Burnstown, 1996.
16. Published Minutes of the South Shore Yacht and Country Club, Canoe Lake, 1953-54.
17. Published Minutes of the Canoe Lake and District Leaseholders Association, 1939 to present.
18. Canoe Lake Duet, Cottage Life, 1998.
19. Interviews with Dan Stringer and Aubrey Dunne by Doug Wyatt and Ottelyn Addison, 1971.
20. Interview with Chuck Matthews, by Rory MacKay, 1975.
21. Interview with Gertrude Baskerville, by Rory MacKay, 1976.
22. Interview with Mary Colson Clare, by Don Standfield, 1992.
23. Interview with Gibby and Lulu Gibson, by Don Standfield 1992.
24. Interview with Adèle "Couchie" Statten Ebbs, by Don Standfield 1992.
25. Notes from Marg McColl and Isobel Cowie, found by James MacDonald, 1998.
26. Thompson Family Log, 1935-1984.
27. Edited transcripts of notes of interviews with Dan Gibson, Hank Laurier, Harvey Loyst, Jim and Catherine Brackley, Sylvia Hayhurst Telford, Marion Cherry, Karen Stringer Ferraris, Karen Bullock, Chuck and Dorothy Gray, Janey Roberts, Isabel Clemson, Marg Hogg, Nick Deciano, Mary Colson Clare, Bill Matthews, Islay McFarlane, Carolyn Fink, Don Lloyd, Sue Ebbs, Viiu Kanep, James MacDonald, Joan Ridpath, John Ridpath, Sherry Sandilands, Jane McWhinney, Cliff and Tamar Nelson, Mary Percival, Carolyn and Bob Phinney.
28. Written stories from Betsy Hogg Cook, Ernie Bilkey, Mary Margaret Armstrong Withey, Sandy Lewis and Isobel Cowie.
29. MacGregor, R., Canoe Lake, A Novel, (originally published as Shorelines in 1980), McClelland & Stewart, Toronto 2002.

ISBN 1553694899-9

9 781553 694892